D0543909

Alan Dupont

The Environment and Security in Pacific Asia

DISCARDED FROM STOCK

Adelphi Paper 319

Oxford University Press, Great Clarendon Street, Oxford OX2 6DP
Oxford New York
Athens Auckland Bangkok Bombay Calcutta Cape Town
Dar es Salaam Delhi Florence Hong Kong Istanbul Karachi
Kuala Lumpur Madras Madrid Melbourne Mexico City
Nairobi Paris Singapore Taipei Tokyo Toronto
and associated companies in
Berlin Ibadan

Oxford is a trade mark of Oxford University Press

Published in the United States
by Oxford University Press Inc., New York

© The International Institute for Strategic Studies 1998

First published June 1998 by **Oxford University Press** for
The International Institute for Strategic Studies
23 Tavistock Street, London WC2E 7NQ

Director John Chipman
Editor Gerald Segal
Assistant Editor Matthew Foley
Design and Production Mark Taylor

British Library Cataloguing in Publication Data
Data available

Library of Congress Cataloguing in Publication Data

ISBN 0-19-922370-X
ISSN 0567-932X

Staffordshire
UNIVERSITY

Library and Information Service

contents

maps & tables

Unresolved territorial disputes, divided countries and an uncertain balance of power are some of the many reasons to worry about the future security of Pacific Asia. Since the early 1990s, concern has also grown that environmental problems are threatening regional security. Worried analysts have written of the risks to stability posed by disputes over pollution, water, food and energy resources and mass migration. But are these issues relevant to the region's security climate? To what extent – if at all – do environmental issues shape the security agenda?

At first glance, environmental issues would seem to be a priority for the people and governments of Pacific Asia. Acrid smoke from the fires which raged across the Indonesian islands of Sumatra and Kalimantan in 1997 and 1998 – delicately called a 'haze' – had significant economic repercussions for the region as a whole. It also cast a political pall over Indonesia's relations with its closer neighbours in the Association of South-East Asian Nations (ASEAN), lending credence to the environmentalists' view that ecological damage is becoming a significant potential cause of conflict. This is seen to be particularly the case in the developing world where, it is argued, environmental damage is undermining the institutions and capabilities of states and creating new types of resource scarcity to do with air, water, fish and forests.[1]

Many analysts, on the other hand, doubt that environmental degradation can lead to serious conflict, and argue that it is difficult to identify specific links between environmental problems and major threats to security.[2] Sceptics include those who see the region's overall security climate as largely benign, and those who take a less sanguine view, but are concerned primarily with more 'traditional' issues such as territorial disputes and balance-of-power politics.

The considerable confusion over the exact nature of the links between environmental and security issues, together with the imprecise and frequently arbitrary use of the term 'environmental security', have fostered neither conceptual nor operational clarity and complicate attempts to investigate the debate.[3] A bewildering number of subjects have been labelled as 'environmental security' issues. These include acid rain, agricultural yields, biodiversity, deforestation, economic competitiveness, flooding, fossil fuels, global warming, hazardous waste, infectious diseases, refugees, illegal migration, oil crises, over-population, poverty, soil degradation, sustainable development, trans-boundary pollution and urbanisation.[4]

Environmental security embraces three distinct schools of thought. The first, which is most common in national-security establishments, focuses on the use of military forces to monitor environmental change and to assist in protecting or rejuvenating the environment.[5] The second aspect is environmental warfare – the explicit targeting of an adversary state's resources or physical environment in a bid to degrade or destroy its capacity to wage war.[6] A third category, and that with which this study is primarily concerned, defines environmental security in terms of 'acute' sub-national or international conflict with a substantial probability of violence or the prospect of serious political and social instability stemming from human activities which reduce the environment's capacity to sustain life.[7] This broad definition covers a range of issues. In order to narrow down precisely which environmental issues have an impact on security, it is necessary to move beyond theoretical debates and focus on the evidence provided by case-studies and practical examples.

is there a causal link between environment and security?

This paper asks whether there is a causal link between environmental degradation, resource scarcity and conflict.[8] There are particular reasons to focus on environmental security in Pacific Asia (South-east and North-east Asia). The region is home to a third

Map I *Pacific Asia*

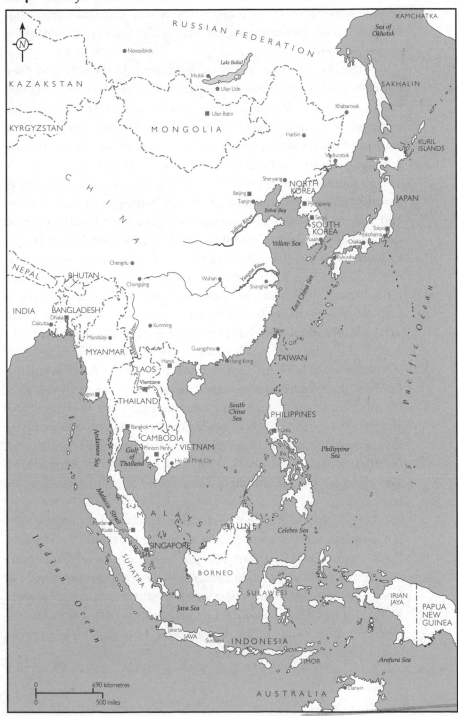

of the world's population and is overwhelmingly comprised of developing states – those countries which Canadian academic Thomas Homer-Dixon argues are most at risk from environmentally generated conflict.[9]

The aim of this study is twofold: first, to identify and shed light on those environmental factors which are already affecting Pacific Asia's security; and second, to analyse how and under what circumstances environmental factors interact with other sources of conflict to exacerbate, prolong or complicate existing disputes and national-security problems. The debate about the importance of environmental issues is to some extent a debate about the *meaning* of security. Shifts in the balance of power, competing belief systems and the preservation of sovereignty figure prominently in most explanations of conflict. A host of other variables are, however, also at work. Most of the world's major armed conflicts of the past decade, including in Pacific Asia, have been internal, rather than international.[10] This is precisely the area where environmental factors are most likely to affect security, in association with other, more familiar domestic challenges. While ecological pressure may not be the principal, direct or even ostensible cause of military conflict, it is having a discernible impact on Pacific Asia's security – far more than traditional security analyses have generally allowed. On the other hand, some environmentalists have been guilty of alarmist talk of the effects of ecological degradation, conjuring up images of environmental breakdown leading to violent conflict and, eventually, social and political anarchy in the developing world. The effect of the environment on security is considerably more complex.

This paper argues that environmental issues are unlikely to be the primary cause of a major conflict between states. Nonetheless, these issues are important because they are among the more significant causes of certain conflicts. The environmental fall-out from the Indonesian fires damaged political relations between ASEAN states. Environmental factors can thus play a significant – albeit complex – role in shaping relations among states in general, and regional security in particular.

Staffordshire University
CheckOut Receipt

Issued on:
09/04/09
19:51

Item:Social choice and public policy.
30121002099586
Due for return on:
24/04/09

Item:Welfare theory and social policy :
reform or revolution? /
30121002484259
Due for return on:
24/04/09

Item:Power in caring professions.
30121003605175
Due for return on:
24/04/09

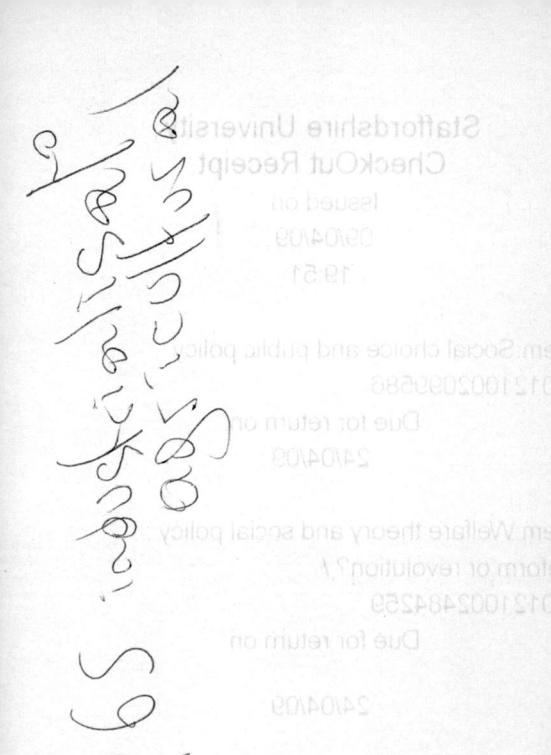

chapter 1

Pollution and Conflict

South-east Asia's Forest Fires

The choking smog which enveloped large areas of South-east Asia in the latter half of 1997 and early 1998 was an environmental disaster for the region with few modern parallels in terms of its scale and political impact. The pollution – the result of unusually severe forest fires on the Indonesian islands of Sumatra and Kalimantan – affected the health of at least 20 million Indonesians and strained relations between Jakarta and its ASEAN neighbours. The smog also had significant political, health and economic repercussions for Brunei, Malaysia, the Philippines and Thailand.

Fire is an intrinsic part of the life-cycle of Indonesia's forests, but the 1997–98 blazes were an act of man, not nature. The destruction of forests in Kalimantan, Sumatra and, to a lesser extent, Irian Jaya and Sulawesi, began in earnest in the 1970s. It has accelerated in the 1990s following the Indonesian government's decision to increase palm-oil production significantly. Since 1985, the area of land given over to palm-oil plantations has grown from 600,000 hectares to 2.2m ha; a further 3.3m ha is scheduled to be planted by 2000. Jakarta, which earned $1 billion in 1996 from these plantations, aims to make Indonesia the world's largest producer by 2005.[1]

Forest-burning in Indonesia is the cheapest and quickest method of clearing land for palm-oil plantations. Fires lit by plantation owners on Kalimantan in 1994 created one of the worst smogs in Indonesia before 1997, forcing airports and other facilities on Kalimantan and nearby Sulawesi to close for several weeks. Pollution in Singapore reached unprecedented levels, Malaysia declared a public alert and both countries sought urgent talks with Indonesia on cross-border atmospheric pollution.[2]

Two factors – a severe drought caused by the *El Niño* weather system and the presence of carcinogenic particles in the smog – conspired to increase significantly the environmental impact of the fires of 1997. The fires spread out of control, and prevailing winds carried a cloud of dense pollution as far as northern Australia.[3] Malaysia and Singapore recorded their highest-ever levels of atmospheric pollution.[4] The smoke disrupted transport and contributed to at least two serious accidents. Factories, schools, air and sea ports, government offices and other key facilities on Kalimantan and Sumatra were closed for extended periods and Sarawak declared a state of emergency on 19 September. Economic losses from reduced manufacturing and agricultural output were compounded by a sharp decline in tourism.[5] Reduced sunlight impeded the growth of palm-oil plantations in Indonesia and Malaysia.[6] The economic costs of the fires for Indonesia, Malaysia and Singapore was conservatively estimated at $1.4bn in short-term health care, lost tourist revenue and reduced industrial and agricultural production.[7] Continued burning throughout 1998 would, it was estimated, cost these countries up to $6bn – equivalent to 2.5% of their combined gross domestic product (GDP).[8]

The political costs for Indonesia were equally high. Although initially blaming the fires on natural causes – principally *El Niño* – then President Suharto was forced to issue two unprecedented apologies to neighbouring states in September and October. On 6 October, Environment Minister Sarwono Kusumaatmadja acknowledged that 'if we don't change our ways, we won't survive as a nation. I hope this time we make doubly sure [the fires] won't happen again, otherwise we'll be out of business forever'.[9] Discontent and anger among Indonesia's normally respectful ASEAN neighbours deepened as the smog worsened. Malaysia's opposition leader, Lim Kit Siang, moved an emergency motion on 28 September calling for a parliamentary debate on Indonesia's failure to put out the fires.[10] Environment Minister Law Hieng Din chided Indonesian officials for their lack of effective action.[11] Thailand's *Nation* daily newspaper

the political damage from the Indonesian fires

blamed Jakarta for providing logging companies with subsidies to clear forests, and asked: 'who is to pay for this wanton act of destruction, if not the people of Southeast Asia?'.[12] Singapore's Environment Minister, Yeo Cheow Tong, politely but pointedly reminded Indonesia that the fires could not be allowed to burn out of control.[13]

The Indonesian fires are a reminder of the dangers of ignoring the lessons of sustainable economic development. Systematic abuse of the region's natural resources is causing air, water and ground pollution on such a scale that, in 1997, the Asian Development Bank (ADB) labelled Asia 'the world's most polluted and environmentally degraded region'.[14]

Air Pollution

Air quality in virtually all the region's major cities has significantly deteriorated since the mid-1970s. According to the World Health Organisation (WHO), nine of the 15 cities with the highest partic-ulate (dust and soot) levels in the world, and six of the 15 worst affected by sulphur dioxide, are in Pacific Asia. Carbon dioxide emissions per unit of GDP in Pacific Asia are three times those of Latin America, and the region is projected to account for more than 50% of the world's incremental growth in carbon dioxide and sulphur dioxide by 2000.[15]

Government attempts to address the air-quality issue have in the main been sporadic, limited and ineffectual. The Malaysian government's disregard for the clean-air recommendations of its own environmental experts is typical of the way in which the region's governments have placed economic development ahead of environmental considerations. Much of the smog which enveloped Kuala Lumpur at the height of the crisis in 1997 came from local industrial and car emissions which the aborted 1994 Clean Air Action Plan was designed to reduce.[16]

Air pollution throughout Pacific Asia is forecast to worsen as more motor vehicles throng the region's streets, especially in China.[17] Unless remedial action is taken, and there is reason to doubt that it will be, economic growth is likely to suffer, with implications for the region's political and social climate.[18] The economic costs of dealing with pollution are only now being recognised. In 1992, the Chinese National Environmental Protection Agency (NEPA) estimated that the effects of acid rain and air and water pollution were costing some 15% of the nation's GDP.[19] China spends just 0.85% of its GDP ($9.7bn) annually on environmental protection.[20] Public tolerance of lax environmental-safety regulations and high pollution levels is falling, even in authoritarian states like China. In mid-1993, public anger in Lanzhou at a chemical plant's persistent breaches of regulatory limits on pollution boiled over into serious rioting.[21]

As the Indonesian fires demonstrate, the consequences of worsening pollution may be felt beyond national jurisdictions. Japan and South Korea are increasingly concerned about the political, economic and health effects of airborne pollutants and acid rain from coal-burning power stations in China. South Korea's air quality is among the worst in the region, and the country suffers from the highest methane concentration – a key cause of global warming – in the world. Ozone warnings threaten to become a routine part of life in Seoul.[22] South Korean researchers are convinced that much of the methane, along with other dangerous chemicals and particulates, originates in China.[23] In Japan, scientists claim that 50% of the country's measured deposits of sulphur dioxide are of Chinese origin (a further 15% is said to come from South Korea).[24]

China has denied responsibility for its neighbours' environmental problems, and neither Seoul nor Tokyo has been prepared to make pollution a major issue.[25] This tolerance is set to be tested in the future as Chinese industrial emissions increase in line with the country's expanding economy and greater use of fossil fuels. China has an estimated 11% of the world's coal reserves; coal provides 75% of the country's commercial energy. With these reserves likely to last for up to 1,000 years, Beijing is almost certain to use them to meet its anticipated energy shortfall. Between 1990 and 2000, electricity generation in China will probably double to 300 gigawatts, 80% from coal-fired plants.[26]

Coal-burning is not the only pollution problem with the potential to harm inter-state relations in North-east Asia. China's plans to build an extensive nuclear-power industry could pose environmental questions for Seoul and Tokyo. A radioactive discharge into the atmosphere could trigger a major adverse public reaction in South Korea and Japan. Pollution has already intruded into the security relationship between Japan and the US. In November 1997, US Navy officials protested to their Japanese counterparts about the fumes blowing over the military base at Atsugi near Tokyo from a large industrial-waste incinerator, and urged that it be shut down. The Navy claimed that the fumes contained a toxic mix of chemicals which was damaging the health of service personnel.[27]

Pollution and the Food Chain

Pollution is seriously affecting Pacific Asia's food chain. Millions of hectares have been polluted, leaving large tracts of arable land infertile. Toxins will be difficult to clean up, and Pacific Asia's record of combating soil pollution compares poorly with that of other developing regions. The problem is particularly acute at sea. Most of Pacific Asia's major cities are located in coastal areas or adjacent to river systems which drain into the sea. As cities expand, coastal regions are being stripped of their protective vegetation and increasing amounts of untreated industrial and human waste are pouring into river estuaries and coastal waters.

Serious marine pollution affects large areas, especially the Gulf of Thailand, Manila and Jakarta Bays, the South China Sea, the Mekong Delta and the waters off China, Japan and South Korea.[28] The over-use of chemical fertilisers to improve crop yields and the rapid increase in shipping have contributed to high levels of pollution in the Yellow, East and South China Seas. Oil carried by rivers from the Beijing area and from ships and offshore drilling platforms has polluted Bohai Bay. In the mid-1980s, at least one-third of China's coastal waters contained significant levels of cadmium, mercury and heavy metals. The situation has worsened since.[29] The lower reaches of the Tumen River in North Korea are also badly polluted.[30]

The East China Sea suffered its first major disaster in November 1971, when the tanker *Juliana* spilled 6,400 tons of oil, devastating fish and other marine life.[31] The break-up of a Russian oil tanker, the *Nakhodka*, off the Japanese coast in January 1997 seriously damaged Japan's sensitive fish and aqua-culture breeding-grounds. The accident also became a contentious political issue between Russia and Japan as the two states argued over who should accept the blame.[32]

Regional governments are concerned that a major oil spill could seriously disrupt or even close the heavily trafficked Malacca Strait.[33] A large-scale spill and subsequent closure of the Strait would have devastating environmental and economic consequences. In the mid-1990s, over 1,100 fully laden oil tankers were passing through the Strait, 'many with only a meter or two of clearance between their keels and the channel bottom'.[34] Indonesia and Malaysia have, since 1993, stepped up cooperation in prosecuting crews dumping oil and waste at sea.[35]

Worsening pollution is the unwanted legacy of Pacific Asia's rapid economic development. There is little doubt that pollution will become a major environmental-policy issue for the region's governments. Although it is unlikely to be a primary cause of military conflict, the regional indignation over the Indonesian fires and the diplomatic difficulty between Japan and the US over the Atsugi incinerator demonstrate that growing sensitivity to pollution will influence the security-policy climate.

Some forms of pollution are more likely than others to have political and security implications. Toxic soils are a long-term social and economic problem for the region, but it is difficult to see this issue having significant security implications. Oil spills can cause political tensions between states, as the *Nakhodka* incident illustrates. A major spill would have significant economic consequences if it took place in a confined sea-lane such as the Malacca Strait, but oil pollution at sea is unlikely to lead to military conflict.

Further fires in Indonesia on the scale of those in 1997–98 and intensified acid rain in North-east Asia – both of which are probable – are the two air-pollution issues most likely to have implications for security and foreign policy because of their high visibility and potentially widespread impact. Even so, the regional response to the Indonesian fires suggests that serious transnational pollution would be most likely to prompt closer cooperation, rather than confrontation. For example, in one of the first serious regional attempts to deal with the fires, ASEAN Environment Ministers agreed in April 1998 to set up a fund to assist in fire-fighting in Indonesia and to 'control and channel additional and complementary resources from the region and internationally'.[36] Pollution should be seen more as a reflection of the economic, social, environmental and demographic forces shaping Pacific Asia's security environment, rather than as a fundamental cause of them.

chapter 2

Population and Conflict

Global Demographic Trends

Two hundred years ago, English economist and demographer Thomas Malthus drew attention to the link between population growth and conflict. Malthus argued that, unless checked by famine, war or ill-health, population increases always tended to outstrip the growth of production.[1] This gloomy prognosis has not been borne out because population growth resulting from advances in health care has been offset by increased agricultural production. Nonetheless, when Malthus made his prediction in 1798, the world's population was less than one billion. A dramatic increase in human fertility rates and fall in mortality rates mean that, by the end of this century, the Earth will support six billion people.

Most demographic forecasts are based on UN projections made in 1992, and revised in 1994 and 1996, showing low, medium and high growth scenarios. According to the 1996 medium-variant projection, the world's population will reach 9.4bn by the middle of the twenty-first century, before stabilising at 11bn people around 2200.[2]

Demographers generally accept this projection.[3] A minority, however, believe that greater credence should be given to the UN's low-variant model.[4] This expects the world population to peak at 7.7bn in 2040 – still a 25% increase in just over 40 years. The high-variant projection, while less likely, also cannot be discounted. It predicts a global population of 8.6bn by 2025 and 11.2bn by 2050.

These disagreements aside, several broad trends are not in doubt. First, the world now supports many more people than at any time in human history. Second, the rate of population increase in the twentieth century is unprecedented: 81m people were added to global population annually between 1990 and 1995, more than half of them in Asia.[5] Although the annual rate of increase has slowed to 1.48% from its peak of 2.1% in the late 1960s, world population will continue to grow well into the next century. This is a key point that is often ignored or under-emphasised.[6] Third, these changes have been accompanied by high rates of urbanisation: according to the UN, 43% of the world's population lived in urban areas in the mid-1990s. By 2015, 4.1bn of the world's estimated population of 7.3bn will be city-dwellers. Ninety-seven per cent of the increase in the world's population will take place in the developing world. Two-thirds of that growth will occur in cities.[7]

Pessimists argue that the Earth will be unable to support a substantially higher and denser population without radical changes in attitudes to economic growth, consumption and energy use. Optimists, on the other hand, believe that the Earth has sufficient ecological and physical resilience to withstand growing population pressures, and reject the Malthusian idea that famine and conflict inevitably follow from population increases.[8]

The truth lies midway between these two points of view. There is no direct link between population growth and conflict. If there were, the latter half of the twentieth century should have been a significantly more violent period than earlier times, when both the rate of population growth and population levels were lower. This is not the case: even the most brutal internecine wars of the late twentieth century do not compare with the global conflicts of 1914–18 and 1939–45. Nonetheless, the rapid growth in global population is beginning to reduce the availability and quality of natural resources and living space. Global stocks of fresh water are declining as demand rises and pollution and urbanisation increase. Productive agricultural land is being eroded or given over to urban development, deforestation is proceeding apace and many animal and marine habitats are under threat.

High levels of population growth are an additional burden on governments, particularly those in developing countries where fragile national institutions and the social fabric may already be threatened by ethnic, religious or other sub-national sources of tension. High levels of unemployment fuel political discontent and social dislocation. Economic distortions are growing as states with rising populations find it more difficult to eliminate income inequalities and to sustain rates of economic growth sufficient to absorb excess labour. Population pressure and environmental degradation are responsible for large-scale movements of people, both within states and across borders. These unregulated flows are becoming a significant potential source of conflict in many parts of the developing world, including Pacific Asia.[9]

Population Growth in Pacific Asia

With the exception of Japan, Singapore and South Korea, populations across Pacific Asia are substantially increasing.[10] The region will be home to over two billion people by 2000, or just under one-third of the world's total population. By 2025 Pacific Asia could contain almost 2.5bn people, of whom 1.5bn will live in China (see Table 1, page 20).[11]

Pacific Asia has seven of the world's 14 largest cities and, by 2000, it will have eight cities with populations of over ten million.[12] This is a significant development for the previously rural and agrarian societies of the region. In 1950, 58m of Asia's people lived in cities with populations of over one million. Forty years later, that figure had swelled to 359m – more than Europe and North America combined.[13] Asia will probably host half of the world's urban population by 2025 (see Table 2, page 21).[14] This increase will be a primary cause of environmental degradation as cities strain to cope with the infrastructural and social demands of rapid influxes of people.

Over-population and urbanisation are most evident in Pacific Asia's two most populous states, China and Indonesia, which between them will account for three-quarters of the region's population by 2025. Despite two of the best-run and most generously funded population-control programmes in the developing world, experts in both countries concede that their populations will soar above desirable levels before declining to more manageable proportions in about another 100 years.[15]

Table 1 *Population Growth in Pacific Asia (millions), 1992–2025*

	1992	2000	2025	Percentage change, 2000/2025
North-east Asia				
China[a]	1,182.7	1,299.0	1,513.0	16%
(Hong Kong	6.0	6.5	6.5	0)
Japan	124.0	128.5	127.5	-0.8
South Korea	44.0	46.4	51.6	11
North Korea	23.1	26.1	33.1	27
Total	**1,379.8**	**1,506.5**	**1,731.7**	**15**
South-east Asia				
Indonesia	184.0	219.6	287.0	31%
Vietnam	71.1	82.4	117.5	43
Philippines	64.0	77.5	111.5	44
Thailand	58.0	63.7	80.9	27
Myanmar	44.5[b]	51.1	72.6	42
Malaysia	19.0	22.0	30.1	37
Cambodia	9.1	10.5	14.0	33
Laos	4.6	5.5	8.6	56
Singapore	3.0	3.0	3.3	10
Brunei	0.3	0.3	0.4	33
Total	**457.6**	**535.6**	**725.9**	**36**
Total (Pacific Asia)	**1,837.4**	**2,042.1**	**2,457.6**	**20**

Notes   [a] Chinese figures include those for Taiwan

        [b] Estimated

Sources   Projections for 2000 and 2025: *World Bank Atlas 1996* (Washington DC: The World Bank, 1995). 1992 figures: *Asia 1995 Yearbook* (Hong Kong: Far Eastern Economic Review, 1994); *The Military Balance 1993–1994* (London: Brassey's for the IISS, 1993)

Table 2 *Proportion of Urban Populations in Pacific Asia, 1990–2025*

	1990	2000	2025
Singapore	100.0%	100.0%	100.0%
Japan	77.2	78.4	84.9
South Korea	73.8	86.2	93.7
North Korea	59.8	63.1	75.2
Brunei	57.7	59.0	72.5
Malaysia	49.8	57.5	72.7
Philippines	48.8	59.0	74.3
Indonesia	30.6	40.3	60.7
China	26.2	34.5	54.5
(Hong Kong	94.1	95.7	97.3)
Myanmar	24.8	28.4	47.3
Vietnam	19.9	22.3	39.1
Thailand	18.7	21.9	39.1
Laos	18.6	25.1	44.5
Cambodia	17.6	24.1	43.5
East Timor	7.8	7.5	14.4
Total	48.1	54.5	68.8

Source *World Urbanization Prospects: The 1994 Revision* (New York: United Nations, 1995), Table A.2, p. 81

China

The size of China's population and its rate of increase over the past 50 years are key strategic issues for the country's government. Between 1950 and 1990, China's population grew by 571m people. From 1990 to 2020, the country will expand by close to 490m – the equivalent of another South-east Asia. Its projected population of 1.5bn in 2017 will near that of the total *world* population in 1900.[16] As Lester Brown observes, merely to feed, house and clothe this many extra people in such a short time poses formidable problems for the Chinese government and will further degrade the country's environment. China cannot take advantage of migration to control population levels, nor does it have readily accessible virgin land to accommodate the scale of population growth it faces.[17]

STAFFORDSHIRE UNIVERSITY LIBRARY

Population growth and urbanisation are important factors in the rising level of violence and lawlessness in China.[18] The country's expanding cities attract criminal groups trading in drugs, people and contraband.[19] Illegal migration from China has in the 1990s become a significant source of friction with other Pacific states, notably Japan and the US.[20] High levels of population growth also erode the benefits of economic development and modernisation. According to the semi-official *Beijing Review*:

> unless population growth is curbed, China's increase in wealth will be offset by the ever-larger number of people who have to share it ... as the contradiction between population and resources grows, environmental deterioration will follow.[21]

Indonesia

Indonesia's population of 200m will expand to 340m by the end of the next century – more than North America's population in 1998 and half that of Europe.[22] High levels of economic and population growth and unparalleled pressure on the country's urban and rural environments are eroding the country's economic gains and undermining the regime.

Indonesia's expanding population could become a security issue in areas where pre-existing social, ethnic and religious tensions are also increasing. For this reason, large populations are increasingly seen as a strategic liability, rather than the hallmark of a great power. The distribution, rather than absolute size, of the population is the key issue. Well over half the population – 117m people – lives

population growth and the risk of communal tension

on Java, the smallest of Indonesia's five major islands and one of the most densely populated areas in the world. Java suffers from many of the population ills of coastal China and other areas of comparable population density in Pacific Asia. The government has encouraged Javanese farmers to relocate to the relatively under-populated outer islands, including Irian Jaya, through the 'Go East' transmigration and development programme launched in 1990.[23] So many ethnic Javanese and other nonindigenous ethnic groups have flooded into Irian Jaya that, in some areas, they outnumber the local Melanesians.[24]

The presence of large numbers of Javanese and other non-Melanesian ethnic groups has exacerbated long-standing communal problems in Irian Jaya. Violence flared between the island's ethnic communities in late 1995 and 1996; keen to capitalise on local grievances, the separatist Free Papua Movement (OPM) became involved in several clashes with government forces. The violence was sparked by a range of issues, including land rights, the environment, ethnic differences and hostility towards US mining firm PT Freeport Indonesia, the largest foreign company operating in Irian Jaya.[25] However, a significant underlying cause of the unrest was the hostility between indigenous tribes and Javanese newcomers.[26]

Events in Irian Jaya demonstrate how population growth can exacerbate pre-existing social problems such as ethnic tension and unemployment. As a result of the region's financial crisis of 1997–98, some two million casual workers in the Jakarta area lost their jobs between August and December 1997. These redundancies prompted a warning from the armed forces that the country's stability was at risk if high unemployment persisted.[27]

The link between population and conflict is complex, and, since other associated factors – energy, food and water availability, for example – are usually present, it cannot be argued that population increase is a direct or inevitable cause of conflict. As Norman Myers observes, population growth is essentially 'conflict neutral' until it reaches such proportions that it overstretches the 'capacities of the natural resource base to sustain it, and the capacities of governments and other institutions to accommodate it'.[28] Nonetheless, rapid population growth, especially in urban areas, will increasingly test the institutional strength and social cohesion of Pacific Asia's developing states and place further pressure on the region's fragile ecosystems.

chapter 3

Energy Scarcity

Gaining access to vital raw materials has long occupied national-security planners: nations have fought for control of scarce natural resources at least as far back as the Trojan War.[1] For much of the twentieth century, securing control over oil and other non-renewable energy resources has been a central strategic objective of the great powers. Historians Paul Kennedy and Jonathan Martin have shown that competition for raw materials was an important element of inter-state conflict and national power well before the environment entered the lexicon of international security.[2] Almost 80 years ago, French Senator Henri Berenger claimed that 'who has oil has empire', foreshadowing an extended period of strategic rivalry over oil between the powers of his day.[3]

Berenger and his generation believed that oil was the lubricant of empire and the natural inheritance of the strong. In the past, access to and control over oil have tended to be seen as measures of national strength. While this view still underpins the approach of some nations to energy resources, the acquisitive impulses of earlier years are weakening. Acquiring strategic minerals by military conquest has become far less attractive, and using political manipulation or economic pressure has become more difficult. In addition, governments are beginning to appreciate that certain kinds of energy use will incur political, social and environmental costs which may have implications for national security.

A second important difference in the modern approach to energy resources is that environmental damage is creating new kinds of resource scarcity. So-called 'renewable resources' such as fish and water are being exploited to such an extent that they are becoming 'functionally non-renewable'.[4] This erosion of primary renewable resources differentiates modern resource scarcity from that of the past. Despite progress in developing substitutes for the non-renewable resources which have historically been a cause of conflict, there are few alternatives to renewable ones.

In Pacific Asia, resource scarcity is aggravating tensions over unresolved maritime-boundary quarrels. Every state in the region except land-locked Laos is involved in at least one dispute with a neighbour (see Map 2, page 32). Disputes at sea have led to military confrontation, or have been the subject of official protests. What is new and troubling about these disputes is that they are taking place against a background of rising energy demand, high economic growth and diminishing energy self-sufficiency on an unprecedented scale.

Energy in Pacific Asia

The drive to find and exploit new sources of energy at sea is linked to anxieties over how to secure stable and affordable long-term energy supplies. Before the economic crisis took hold in the latter half of 1997, the region's economies were doubling in size approximately every decade, and its energy use was increasing by factors of between five and ten.[5] Pre-crisis forecasts estimated that, between 1996 and 2010, Pacific Asia's share of global energy demand would rise from 13% to 28%, a growth rate almost twice that of the rest of the world combined.[6]

The severity of the 1997–98 economic downturn, arguably the region's worst since the 1930s, will result in a significant reduction in energy demand until at least 2000. Nonetheless, there is general agreement among energy experts that pre-crisis forecasts of long-term rises in energy demand remain valid. Even assuming that the rate of growth in the demand for oil drops from 5.2% (the 1990–95 average) to 1% between 1998 and 2000, and averages only 4% a year thereafter, by 2010 the regional demand for oil would still be nine million barrels per day (bpd) higher than in 1996. This increase is greater than Saudi Arabia's current output of oil.[7]

Table 3 *Growth in Primary Energy Demand in Pacific Asia, 1995–1997*

	1995[a]	1996	1997[b]
Malaysia	10.9%	9.8%	8.6%
Thailand	10.7	12.4	10.9
Myanmar	9.7	6.1	5.9
Vietnam	9.2	14.7	12.8
South Korea	8.6	9.4	7.3
China	6.0	5.8	5.6
Singapore	5.5	6.0	5.0
Indonesia	4.1	9.0	8.7
Philippines	4.1	6.8	7.8
Taiwan	3.1	4.5	6.2
Brunei	1.7	6.2	6.5
Japan	1.6	2.1	2.5
Average	6.3	7.7	7.3

Notes [a] 1995 figures for South-east Asian countries are an average for the period 1993–95

[b] 1997 figures are pre-economic crisis projections

Source Extrapolated from data in Cambridge Energy Research Associates, *Asia-Pacific Energy Watch*, Winter/Spring 1997

China is likely to record the world's fastest rise in energy consumption in the first decade of the twenty-first century, by which time absolute levels of consumption could equal those of all the European Organisation for Economic Cooperation and Development (OECD) nations combined.[8] In South-east Asia, rapid urbanisation and economic growth in the second tier of 'tiger economies' have resulted in even higher relative increases in demand for electricity. Between 1993 and 1995, electricity generation in Brunei, Indonesia, Malaysia, Myanmar, the Philippines, Thailand and Vietnam rose by, on average, 13% a year.[9] These rises will almost certainly slow significantly in 1998 and 1999. Nevertheless, the demand for electricity is still likely to more than double by 2010 because of continued urbanisation and industrial development and the growth of rural electrification programmes.[10]

Pacific Asia lacks the energy resources to meet its growing needs. The region provides only one-tenth of the world's oil supply and has just one-twentieth (4.42%) of its estimated extractable reserves.[11] Energy self-sufficiency is expected to fall from 43% in 1995 to 29% in 2015, by which time Pacific Asia may have to import as much as 70% of its oil.[12] The region is likely to have to import more than 20m bpd of oil by 2010, compared with 11m bpd in 1997.[13]

This energy imbalance is most pronounced in North-east Asia. Japan imports 88% of its primary energy supplies and 90% of its oil. In 1996, despite an official policy designed to diversify oil suppliers, over 80% of the country's crude oil came from the Middle East – Japan's highest level of import dependence on the Middle East since the first oil crisis of 1972.[14] South Korea's energy dependence is higher still, North Korea has no oil at all and Taiwan has major energy vulnerabilities.[15]

The situation in South-east Asia is more complex. Cambodia, Singapore and Thailand are major energy importers. Laos, Vietnam and, possibly, the Philippines are likely to become modest net exporters, while Indonesia and Malaysia are significant energy suppliers, mainly to the Asian region. But the overall picture is worsening because of accelerating domestic demand, high energy exploration and development costs, political uncertainties associated with some economically exploitable energy deposits and a decline in recoverable oil reserves.[16] Malaysia may become an oil importer early in the twenty-first century, while oil production in Indonesia, the region's largest supplier, has declined to the point where the country is expected to become a net oil importer by 2005.[17] China, although possessing substantial oil reserves, was forced to import supplies in 1993.[18] Beijing is expected to import some 3m bpd by 2000.

Will there be an 'Energy Gap'?

Energy dependency does not necessarily translate into energy insecurity. There is no actual or prospective world oil shortage. Known global petroleum reserves are substantial: 70% of the world's 2.4 trillion barrels of recoverable oil have yet to be used, and at least another 4.6tn barrels could be produced if prices rise.[19] However, Pacific Asia's energy problems will not stem from systemic shortfalls or from physical unavailability, but from short-term supply disruptions – such as those of the 1970s – which cause sharp and unexpected price rises. The resulting economic and political damage can be considerable. The oil crises of the 1970s pushed up inflation and were largely responsible for two global recessions.[20]

Optimists counter that the world is far better prepared for shocks of this sort, and point to the ease with which the market adjusted to the loss of Kuwaiti and Iraqi oil during the 1991 Gulf War. However, unlike Europe or the US, Pacific Asia has no mechanism for allocating energy in an emergency, and few states in the region have national strategic stockpiles of any significance. According to Ken Koyama, Senior Economist at the Institute of Energy Economics in Japan, most of the region's states have little more than running-stocks averaging around 40 days – less than half the OECD average of 89 days of domestic consumption.[21] Stockpiles in China are estimated to cover only 20 days of domestic demand. China and Singapore do not even require oil firms to keep a percentage of their production in the country.

A range of potential constraints on supply could increase oil prices, including political instability or military conflict in supplier countries, sanctions, embargoes and economic, legal, environmental and technical problems. Pipelines are particularly vulnerable to disruption where they cross national jurisdictions and regions with a history of ethnic and religious antagonism. Muslim Uighur separatists in western China could, for example, sabotage China's proposed gas pipeline from Kazakstan to Xinjiang province should their conflict with Beijing escalate.

Second, optimists argue that, if markets are allowed to function efficiently, rising oil prices will force consumers to use cheaper alternatives, or encourage producers to extract oil from areas previously considered uneconomical. Markets are, however, imperfect mechanisms for allocating risk. This is especially so in the developing world where, for social, economic and regulatory reasons, rising oil prices may not prompt the expected response. Free-marketeers frequently ignore the political factors that can affect the elasticity of supply and demand. Maximising the state's control over energy resources is an important security consideration for most Pacific Asian governments. For example, even if the cost of alternative energy were to fall significantly, China would be unlikely for strategic reasons to reduce its reliance on domestic coal.

A related argument is that diversification of energy supplies away from oil is reducing the risk of energy shortfalls and supply disruptions. Oil meets 51% of Pacific Asia's total energy needs, compared to a global average of just 40%.[22] There is considerable scope to develop Pacific Asia's solar

Asian energy markets are not as flexible as they should be

and geothermal energy, coal, nuclear power and substantial natural gas reserves. There are ambitious plans to link Pacific Asian consumers with Russian and Central Asian producers, as well as those within the region itself. At least three major transnational gas-pipeline proposals for North-east Asia are at the planning stage:

- Russia's Vostok Plan, running from Yakutsk via Seoul to Fukuoka in southern Japan;
- Japan's Energy Community Plan, involving China, Japan, South Korea, Russia, Taiwan and the US; and
- China's Energy Silk Route Plan, linking the gas fields of Central Asia with China, Japan and South Korea.[23]

A fourth project, a pipeline from the Siberian town of Irkutsk through the two Koreas to Japan, was approved in October 1997. The project, which will cost $11bn, will provide China, South Korea and Russia with 20m tons of natural gas a year from 2006.[24]

Diversification alone will not, however, solve Pacific Asia's energy problems. The infrastructure costs of some of the larger gas projects are significant, and there is a limit to the extent to which other forms of energy can replace oil. Pacific Asia's future power needs may require up to $600bn of investment annually – over 60% of the world's estimated total power-sector investment – between 1998 and 2008.[25] Given the flight of capital in the wake of the 1997–98 currency crisis, competition for increasingly scarce investment capital will limit the region's ability to develop the alternative sources of energy needed to meet anticipated demand.

The optimists' fourth argument is that advances in energy exploration, extraction and production technology will increase the speed with which reserves can be tapped and marketed. In addition, new environmentally friendly technology, such as that responsible for producing low-sulphur coal, can reduce the political and environmental costs of burning fossil fuels. However, developing Asia cannot afford many of these new technologies – costly emission filters for coal-burning power stations, for example. While technological advances may improve the region's energy imbalance, they are unlikely to redress it.

Maritime Disputes in the South China Sea

Uncertainty over future energy supplies will remain a significant factor in prompting maritime conflict in the Western Pacific. As oil-exploration technology has improved, drilling has become feasible in previously inaccessible offshore sites. Oil industry analysts expect that, over the next decade, at least 40 new offshore oil and gas developments, representing $18bn-worth of investment, will come on-stream in South-east Asia alone, allowing the recovery of more than ten billion barrels of oil equivalent.[26]

The rise to prominence of the dispute over the Spratly Islands in the South China Sea has coincided with seismic surveys and oil-exploration activities which have reinforced the view, at least in the region, that the islands sit astride large deposits of oil and natural gas.[27] China's Geology and Mineral Resources Ministry estimates that the Spratlys area holds 17.7bn tons of oil and natural-gas reserves, considerably more than Kuwait's 13bn.[28] The People's Liberation Army (PLA) has argued that these reserves must be protected from the 'predatory advances' of other states which, it complains, have taken advantage of China's tolerance and restraint.[29] In 1994, the official *China Youth News* noted that 'the South China Sea holds reserves worth US$1 trillion. Once Xinjiang has been developed, this will be the sole area for replacement of resources ... Development southwards is perhaps a strategic orientation that [China] will have to choose'.[30]

Among the states claiming sovereignty over the Spratlys, China and Vietnam in particular are using foreign oil companies to 'stake out' positions in deep-water zones as a precaution against future energy scarcity. The potential for conflict is already apparent. An uneasy stand-off between China and Vietnam, which followed a brief but bloody clash over the Spratlys in 1988, ended in early 1997. In March, China moved the *Kan Tan III* exploration rig to a location about 65 nautical miles off the coast of central Vietnam, where it began drilling for gas.

Map 2 *Maritime Disputes in Pacific Asia*

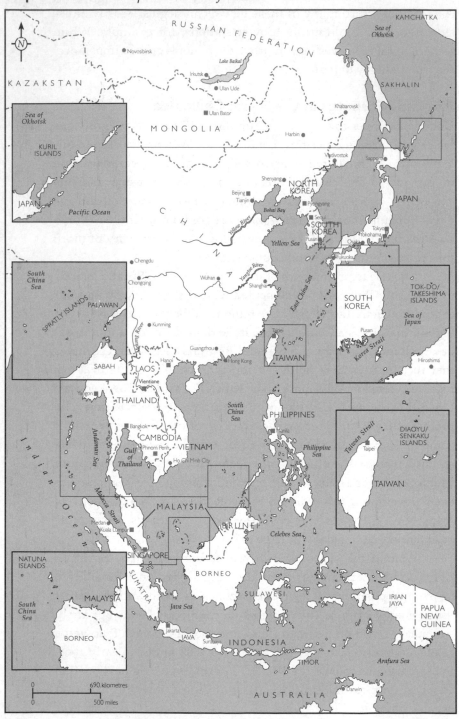

Hanoi, which claimed the area, strongly denied the Chinese Foreign Ministry's assertion that the rig was operating within its rights under international law.[31] The Vietnamese Coast Guard issued repeated warnings to Chinese vessels near the rig. When these were ignored, the official Vietnamese News Agency took the unusual step of publishing extracts of a blunt letter from the government demanding that Beijing 'stop the operation of the Kan Tan III oil rig and withdraw it from the exclusive zone and the continental shelf of Vietnam'.[32] Vietnam also threatened to widen the dispute by soliciting the support of its fellow ASEAN members and, in a bid to raise the strategic stakes, opened discussions with the US on a possible military relationship.[33]

China's aggressive oil-exploration activities in the South China Sea have heightened tensions with ASEAN generally. Indonesia's growing wariness of China's strategic intentions is directly related to concerns that Beijing's territorial claims may overlap with those of Jakarta to the north of the Natunas, a chain of 300 islands and atolls owned by Indonesia to the south of the Spratlys. The Natunas lie above an estimated 1.27tn cubic metres of recoverable gas – one of the world's largest offshore fields – comprising 40% of all Indonesian reserves.[34] In January 1995, Indonesia's state oil company Pertamina and Exxon Corporation of the US signed a $40bn joint venture to exploit the fields. Production is scheduled to begin in 2003 from 18 offshore platforms and six gas-liquefaction trains on Greater Natuna Island.[35]

Two related events illustrate the vulnerability of this massive development project to any future conflict in the South China Sea: the Chinese occupation of the Mischief Reef in the adjacent Spratlys in 1994; and Beijing's publication in 1993 of a map purporting to show the extent of China's territorial claims in the South China Sea. The Chinese boundary appeared to overlap with a portion of Indonesia's Exclusive Economic Zone (EEZ) to the north of the Natunas. In September 1996, the Indonesian Armed Forces staged their biggest-ever exercise in the South China Sea, involving nearly 20,000 troops, 40 aircraft and 50 Naval vessels. A military spokesman described the exercise as 'ensuring security for the development of the mega project in the Natunas'.[36] Given its scope and timing, and despite public statements to the contrary, the exercise was clearly meant to warn China that Indonesia would not tolerate any attempt to encroach upon the Natuna gas-field or Indonesia's contiguous EEZ.[37]

Maritime Disputes in North-east Asia

The perceived need to protect vital resources and to maximise claims to energy-rich contested areas of sea is a major factor in two maritime disputes in North-east Asia. One centres on a group of islands known as the Diaoyu (in Chinese) or Senkaku (in Japanese) located in the middle of the East China Sea. Their ownership is contested by Japan, China and Taiwan. The other is over Tok-do (in Korean) or Takeshima (in Japanese), two tiny islets and a number of scattered shore-reefs in the Sea of Japan almost mid-way between South Korea and Japan, the countries between which ownership is contested.

Both disputes returned to prominence in 1996 following the ratification by China, Japan and South Korea of the 1982 UN Convention on the Law of the Sea (UNCLOS), and each country's subsequent declaration of EEZs of 200 nautical miles.[38] In July, right-wingers from the Japan Youth Foundation built a temporary lighthouse, erected two memorials and planted a flag on the Diaoyu/Senkakus. Two months later, Youth Foundation members returned to repair damage to the lighthouse. The Chinese Foreign Ministry issued a stern warning of 'serious damage' to bilateral relations if Tokyo did not prohibit further similar actions. Anti-Japanese demonstrations broke out in Hong Kong and Taiwan; Taipei charged Beijing with responsibility for protecting Chinese interests in the islands, while five out of six respondents in a Taiwanese newspaper poll called for military action to restore Chinese sovereignty. Tensions eventually eased when both governments realised that the situation could easily develop into a serious confrontation.

The sudden eruption of the Diaoyu/Senkaku dispute illustrates the way in which Pacific Asia's dwindling resources and escalating energy demands are investing the region's remaining renewable and non-renewable stocks with new strategic and economic significance. The Diaoyu/Senkakus are only 7km², and remained relatively obscure until a 1969 study by the UN Economic Commission for Asia and the Far East concluded that the seabed around them could contain one of the richest oil and gas deposits in the world. Later estimates put the oil reserves at between one and ten billion barrels.[39] The islands are particularly important to Japan because, under international law, Tokyo has no other basis for laying claim to a share of the East China Sea continental shelf and its oil deposits.[40]

The potential for military and political conflict over the Diaoyu/Senkakus was apparent even before the 1996 episode. In August 1970, Japan protested against Taiwan's decision to negotiate a contract with the UK's Gulf Oil to prospect for oil in an area that included the islands. In the following month, Japanese police tore down a flag erected by Taiwanese reporters. In December, Beijing lodged a strong claim to ownership of the whole island group. China and Japan agreed to shelve their dispute when relations were normalised in 1972, but periodic incidents continued. China sent some 50 fishing boats to the waters around the islands in 1979 to protest against Japan's construction of a helicopter landing-pad on them.[41]

Competition for energy and other marine resources is largely responsible for the re-emergence and intensification of the Tok-do/Takeshima dispute. The islands themselves, like most others which are contested in maritime Pacific Asia, have no intrinsic value; under Article 121 of UNCLOS, the islands are classified as 'rocks', and therefore not entitled to a 200-nautical mile EEZ. However, ownership would allow either Seoul or Tokyo to use the islands as the basis for claiming a larger share of an area that may contain oil and gas as well as a mineral-rich sea-floor. That these extended claims may overlap with North Korea's EEZ further complicates the issue.[42]

In February 1996, well before the declaration of EEZs, a major diplomatic dispute broke out between Japan and South Korea over Seoul's plans to build a wharf on one of the islands. In response, Japan lodged an official protest, and Foreign Minister Yukihiko Ikeda used a nationally televised news conference to accuse South Korea of infringing Japan's sovereignty. The incident almost led to the cancellation of a scheduled summit before South Korean President Kim Young Sam and Japanese Prime Minister Ryutaro Hashimoto agreed to deal with the issue in subsequent boundary negotiations.[43]

The Nuclear Dimension

Environmental considerations associated with nuclear power, the major energy alternative to crucial non-renewable resources such as oil and coal, further complicate Pacific Asia's energy situation. Energy-poor states like Japan, South Korea and Taiwan embarked on ambitious nuclear energy programmes during the 1960s and 1970s. By the mid-1990s, North-east Asia accounted for approximately 14% of global installed nuclear capacity. Substantial increases are planned by 2010.[44] If these plans are realised, the US Department of Energy forecasts that Pacific Asia could provide up to 48% of the growth in the world's nuclear power sector in 1992–2010.[45]

Other states in the region have announced plans to launch new programmes or to expand existing ones. Between 1992 and 1997, China built three reactors and, by 2020, is expected to be producing 20,000 megawatts from eight plants. North Korea will acquire two 1,000-megawatt South Korean light-water reactors under an agreement between Washington and Pyongyang in October 1994 which established the Korean Peninsula Energy Development Organization (KEDO).[46] In 1997, nuclear power provided 36% of South Korea's electricity; Seoul intends to build 16 new nuclear power plants by 2010 to meet its rising energy needs.[47] In 1998, no power plants operated in South-east Asia, but several ASEAN states have research reactors and Indonesia has seriously considered building up to 12 plants.[48]

Nuclear Waste and Security

While strategic analysts are apt to focus on the weapons potential and proliferation aspects of nuclear power, its environmental-security implications will become increasingly important for Pacific Asia for two principal reasons. First, domestic political sensitivity to the risks of accidental discharges of radioactivity from nuclear-power reactors has increased markedly since the Three Mile Island accident in the US in 1979 and the Chernobyl disaster in Ukraine seven years later. Although originally attractive for its comparatively pristine environmental image, nuclear power is now widely viewed as dirty, dangerous and undesirable. As domestic opposition to nuclear power becomes more entrenched, the potential for violence between states will grow.

Second, waste disposal will become a more pressing political and security issue as the region's consumption of nuclear energy increases and the space at existing storage sites declines. In January 1993, the Japanese government discreetly attempted to ship 1.7 tons of plutonium from France aboard the *Akatsuki Maru* for use in its fast-breeder reactor programme. Before the shipment left France, officials from Indonesia, Malaysia and Singapore expressed concern over reports that it might pass through the Malacca Strait. International and regional protests dogged the ship's journey, even though it took a circuitous course well south of Australia before crossing the Pacific.[49] Later in 1993, Japan demanded that Moscow stop dumping liquid nuclear waste into the Sea of Japan. The protest was unusually sharp, with a senior Foreign Ministry official warning the Russian Ambassador: 'We demand that you stop this kind of dumping. We demand that you never again do this in the future'.[50]

In January 1997, Taiwan announced plans to ship 60,000 tons of low-level waste to North Korea for treatment and storage under a deal expected to be worth $227m to Pyongyang.[51] The agreement prompted an unexpectedly hostile reaction from neighbouring states. South Korea denounced the scheme, claiming that it could turn the Korean Peninsula into a 'death zone'; Foreign Minister Yoo Chong Ha bluntly warned Taipei that Seoul would attempt to block the plan 'by all means'.[52] President Kim Young Sam devoted a major part of his keynote address to the UN-sponsored Earth Summit in June 1997 to the nuclear-waste issue. The South Korean delegation succeeded in inserting a clause into the final document of the UN General Assembly's Special Session on the Earth Summit opposing the 'transboundary' transport of radioactive waste.[53] Taiwan firmly rejected South Korean demands to cancel the deal.[54] China criticised North Korea and Taiwan for ignoring the environmental risks of the scheme and, in a bid to extract maximum political capital from the dispute, offered to take the Taiwanese nuclear waste itself on the grounds that Taiwan was 'an indivisible part of China'.[55]

Environmental Constraints on Energy Use

Environmental considerations could significantly limit the future energy options of governments throughout the region. Indonesia's ambitious nuclear-power plans involve building plants in areas widely regarded as seismically unstable. Despite scepticism from his ministerial colleagues, the support of Baccharuddin Jusuf Habibie, at the time the influential Minister for Science and Technology, appeared to ensure that the project would go ahead.

However, in 1993–97, Indonesian and foreign environmental groups mounted a vigorous campaign against nuclear power. Computer projections showed that an accidental release of radio-active materials from a planned reactor on Java's Muria Peninsula could spread over large areas of South-east Asia and Australia.[56] Due in part to escalating domestic and international pressure, as well as strong opposition from within the government itself, Suharto decided in February 1997 to shelve the plans, designating nuclear power 'an option of last resort'.[57]

Should environmental considerations derail or circumscribe North-east Asia's nuclear energy plans, Japan, South Korea and Taiwan would find it difficult to reduce their high levels of energy dependence. Popular opposition had, by the late 1990s, raised serious doubts about Japan's capacity to achieve its ambitious goals. Without a substantial nuclear component, it is unclear how Japan will develop an 'energy cushion' to insure against future volatility in the supply and price of oil. The country's light-water reactors produce about 35% of its electricity. However, no new plants have come on stream since 1985, and most existing reactors will reach the end of their life-span between 2010 and 2020.[58] The government's 1994 Long Term Program for Nuclear Energy envisaged expanding capacity from 45 to 70 gigawatts by 2010. By late 1997, officials of the Ministry of International Trade and Industry (MITI) had accepted that this target was unrealistic because of opposition from local residents and the anti-nuclear movement.[59]

Public hostility also appears to have complicated efforts to develop and operate plutonium-fuelled fast-breeder reactors intended to meet Japan's long-term energy needs. Japan's plutonium stockpile, which is forecast to reach 70 tons by 2010, has already caused domestic and international political problems.[60] Japanese municipalities are becoming reluctant to store plutonium or other nuclear waste within their boundaries. Neighbouring countries are sensitive to the risk that plutonium might be diverted to produce nuclear weapons.

These examples illustrate that concerns about energy security in Pacific Asia are driven by a complex mix of traditional and emerging factors. They include unprecedented population growth, climbing rates of energy dependence, rapid depletion of existing oil reserves and growing awareness of the environmental costs of increased energy consumption.

energy insecurity is real, albeit exaggerated

Environmental constraints threaten to curtail or at least complicate the energy choices of governments.

Reduced economic growth rates in 1997–98 are likely to dampen energy demand. In addition, attempts to deepen regional cooperation through confidence-building measures and an emerging multilateral security dialogue may allow states to manage tensions over energy resources. However, the fact remains that the increasing incidence of conflict at sea is due, in part, to the growing competition for oil and gas. Inter-state tensions over the disposal of nuclear waste in North-east Asia underline the growing capacity of a new class of energy-related environmental-security issues to aggravate conflict, especially when bilateral relations are already under pressure from other political and strategic rivalries.

chapter 4

Food Scarcity

Global Food Security Concerns

Food, like the soil, water and atmosphere that sustain it, is a renewable resource. As with all resources, food is linked to security when it becomes scarce. In the 1960s and 1970s, much of the literature on food as a security issue focused on the perceived gap between future global production and consumption. As populations increased in developing countries and incomes grew in wealthy ones, it was argued that more grain would be needed, both as a food staple and to feed the growing demand for animal protein associated with more affluent diets. If these demands could not be met, violent conflict over diminishing food supplies would result. The possibility that food-rich states would use food as a 'weapon' in pursuit of foreign-policy goals was also frequently canvassed.[1]

Much of this anxiety over food scarcity dissipated between the mid-1970s and mid-1990s as the revolution in agricultural practices unfolded in the developing world. Food production outpaced population growth by 20% in 1960–90, causing average food prices to fall by 60% in the same period.[2] The seafood catch rose from 22m to some 100m tons between 1950 and 1990, while grain production virtually tripled from 631m to 1,780m tons (see Table 4, page 42).[3]

However, just when it seemed that advances in food technology and production had removed the threat of global famine, food security has again become an important issue. In 1994, barely four years after record global grain and marine harvests, the UN warned that:

> by the year 2050, global demand for food may be three times greater than today. Moreover, during the past two decades the production growth rate has declined, dropping from 3 percent annually during the 1960s, to 2.4 percent in the 1970s and finally to 2.2 percent in the 1980s. In 1991, global agricultural production actually fell, the first decline since 1983.[4]

The Food and Agriculture Organisation (FAO) reported in 1996 that per capita food production had declined in over 50 developing countries since the mid-1970s, while food imports had increased.[5] In the same year, the FAO's Rome Food Summit reminded the international community that some 840m of the world's 5.8bn people still suffered from malnutrition.[6] Without more determined action, 680m people are forecast to be without sufficient food to meet their basic nutritional needs by 2015.[7] As if to reinforce these warnings, world grain stocks fell to their lowest recorded level – 13% of annual consumption – in 1996. While this fall is the result primarily of short-term and probably reversible factors, grain stocks are the world's first level of defence against short-term supply fluctuations.[8]

Population pressures account for some of the decline in per capita food production, while rising living standards have increased the overall demand for food, especially grain. By the late 1990s, crop-yield increases had begun to level off as technology was diverted to higher-priority areas, such as information technology, telecom-

Table 4 *World Seafood Catch and Grain Output, 1950–2030 (million tons)*

	1950	1990	2030[a]
Seafood Catch	22	100	100
Grain Output	631	1,780	2,149

Note   [a] Projected

Source   Lester Brown, *Who Will Feed China?: Wake-up Call for a Small Planet* (London: Earthscan Publications, 1995), p. 126

Table 5 *Net Grain Imports/Exports, 1950–1990 (million tons)*

	1950	1960	1970	1980	1990
North America	23	39	56	130	110
Australia } New Zealand	3	6	8	19	14
Latin America	1	0	4	-15	-10
Eastern Europe } Soviet Union	0	0	-2	-44	-35
Africa	0	-2	-4	-17	-25
Asia	-6	-17	-37	-63	-81
Western Europe	-22	-25	-22	-9	27

Note   Negative figures represent net imports

Source   Brown, *Who Will Feed China?*, p. 105

munications and urban infrastructure, just as the first 'green revolution' had largely run its course. In addition, there is strong evidence to suggest that environmental degradation has played a central role. Environmental damage is reducing global 'carrying capacity' – defined by Paul Ehrlich as 'the number of people that the planet can support without irreversibly reducing its capacity to support people in the future'.[9] Rampant commercial and industrial development, soil erosion and loss of soil fertility through over-logging and intensive pesticide use, for example, have led to the steady disappearance of farmland. It has been estimated that nearly half the 29m tons of grain gained every year from advances in technology and investment in irrigation and fertilisers is lost through environmental degradation.[10] Since 1981, the global area given over to grain production has shrunk by 55m ha to 680m ha, while the per capita grain area has halved.[11] Protein derived from fish and other marine resources is under threat from pollution and over-fishing. Less water is available because of falling water tables and the insatiable demand of urban dwellers and industry for fresh water.

Pacific Asia's Food Situation

Much of the pressure on world food supplies is coming from Pacific Asia. The region's rice yields, which showed a healthy improvement

Table 6 *Arable Land Area in Pacific Asia, 1990–1995*

('ooo ha)	1990	1995	% change
China	93,287	91,977	-1.4
Indonesia	20,253	17,130	-15.4
Thailand	17,494	17,085	-2.3
Myanmar	9,567	9,540	-0.3
Philippines	5,480	5,520	0.7
Vietnam	5,339	5,509	3.1
Japan	4,121	3,970	-3.7
Cambodia	3,755	3,819	1.7
South Korea	1,953	1,787	-8.5
North Korea	1,700	1,700	0
Malaysia	1,700	1,820	7.1
Laos	838	875	4.4
Hong Kong	6	6	0
Brunei	3	3	0
Singapore	1	1	0
Total	**165,497**	**160,742**	**-2.9**

Source   Food and Agriculture Organisation (FAO), www.fao.org

during the 1970s, have since levelled off or declined.[12] In 1996, the Philippines government warned that the country's population growth would outpace its rice production by 2000. Domestic short-falls have forced Manila to import an average of 310,000 tons of rice annually since the late 1980s.[13] Indonesia, once the world's largest rice importer, became self-sufficient in 1984, but ten years later, and despite a record harvest, was again forced to begin importing sup-plies.[14] North Korea faces chronic food shortages as its economy disintegrates.

Fears about the impact of China's rising demand on world grain markets lie at the heart of the debate over food security in Pacific Asia. Lester Brown, the iconoclastic president of the Wash-ington-based Worldwatch Institute, argues that China may soon emerge as 'an importer of massive quantities of grain – quantities so large that they could trigger unprecedented rises in world food prices'. As China's consumption patterns change and the Chinese eat more livestock products and grain, subsequent price rises will overwhelm global markets, causing widespread shortages and 'an unprecedented degree of insecurity', especially in the developing world.[15] Thus, food scarcity, 'rather than military aggression', will become the principal threat to security.[16]

In support of these conclusions, Brown points to the four-fold expansion of China's economy since 1979. The country is beginning to follow the same pattern of consumption as wealthier Japan, South Korea and Taiwan, all of which diversified away from a starch staple – rice – to a diet that included much greater consumption of meat, eggs, milk and other livestock products. However, it takes two kilograms of feed-grain to produce a kilogram of poultry; pork requires four kilograms of feed and beef needs seven. Brown calculates that, if China's 1.2bn people eat more of these products, as seems likely, the country's grain imports will outstrip the world's exportable level of grain, driving prices up: 'In an integrated world economy, China's rising food prices will become the world's rising food prices. China's land scarcity will become everyone's land scarcity'.[17]

Czech economist Vaclav Smil has documented in considerable detail China's loss of farmland to environmental degradation. Smil calculates that 40m ha of farmland has been denuded since the 1950s, approximately the equivalent of all the fields in Argentina and enough to feed 350m people.[18] With one-fifth of the world's population but only one-fifteenth of its arable land, China can ill afford losses of this magnitude. Changing farming practices, such as substituting synthetic chemicals for natural fertilisers, have exacerbated the problem by moving 'China's agroecosystem further away from sustainable practices'.[19] Even Beijing concedes that 'a land crisis is approaching' as farmland loss reaches record levels.[20] In February 1995, Jiang Chunyun, a member of the Communist Party Central Committee, conceded that:

> *In the long run, China's agriculture faces, on the one hand, the tremendous pressure of population growth and fast improvement in living standards and industrialization and, on the other, the severe restrictions imposed by a dwindling farmland, shortages of water resources, and a weak infra-structure.*[21]

Is a Food Crisis Likely?

Although recognising that ensuring sufficient food production is a
long-term challenge, the Chinese government has hotly disputed
Brown's contention that the country is on the verge of a food crisis.
Spokesmen have complained that Brown's arguments are merely a
further example of the West's reluctance to come to terms with
China's rising power.[22] Agriculture Minister Liu Jiang argued in 1996
that the country would be able to feed itself, even with a population
of 1.6bn, by increasing farmers' profits and raising productivity.[23]

*China claims
it can feed itself*

Brown's focus on trends in grain
production obscures the fact that
China has been a net exporter of
food since the mid-1980s, more than
offsetting its grain imports. The country's net food exports were
valued at $2.3bn in 1985 and had increased to $3.8bn by 1995.[24] By
the mid-1990s, China imported 0.4% of its annual grain require-
ments, down from 3% in the early 1980s.

There is therefore considerable reason to question the worst-
case predictions of a major food crisis developing in China and other
Pacific Asian states. Given sufficient political will by governments,
and financial incentives for farmers, shortfalls in food production
could be avoided. Advances in genetic engineering promise a new
generation of high-yield crops extremely resistant to pests and
insects.[25] Relatively small changes in land-management practice can
reap disproportionate improvements in grain yields. The US
Department of Agriculture has argued that, were China to adopt
world-class technology, it could improve yields by as much as 30%.[26]
A 1996 Chinese government White Paper estimated that 10% of the
nation's grain crop was being lost due to mishandling and
inefficiencies in administration and distribution; other analyses put
the losses as high as 30%. Beijing hopes to halve these losses, re-
claiming 20m tons for consumption by 2030.

The FAO estimates that Pacific Asia should be able to meet
anticipated food shortfalls by increasing production and earning
sufficient foreign exchange to import the rest. However, as Canadian
economist Brian Hunter points out, the FAO's food projections are
particularly sensitive to the assumptions on which they are based.
For example, a 10% fall in expected wheat yields, or a 20% increase
in rates of population growth, would probably result in a 30% rise in

the cost of wheat. The FAO forecasts also assume stronger environmental standards and changes in farming practices, neither of which will necessarily take place.[27]

Furthermore, political and security considerations may limit the capacity and willingness of Pacific Asian states to import food, while governments may decide to subsidise uncompetitive domestic producers. Japan, although an inefficient producer of many primary foodstuffs, has resisted fully opening its agricultural markets for domestic political reasons. Asian states equate minimum levels of food self-sufficiency with national security. Food security is one of Japan's six major policies designed to achieve comprehensive national security.[28] Pacific Asia's approach to food is further complicated by its symbolic and cultural importance. Rice is seen by many Asians as possessing a 'spiritual' quality that transcends its simple nutritional function.

It is unclear whether the more optimistic forecasts of Pacific Asia's future food production have adequately taken into account the detrimental effects of environmental degradation. More than a quarter of Asian farmland is either moderately or severely degraded – 'the victim of overcultivation, soil erosion, salinization of irrigated lands, and desertification'.[29] Expanding the area of the region's cultivated land would, however, add little to levels of food production. The key is to improve yields by using biotechnology and environmentally sustainable agricultural practices. On the whole, Pacific Asian governments have a poor track record in both these areas, and there is little sign that biotechnology is on the verge of creating another 'green revolution'.[30]

Food Shortages in North Korea

Even localised and relatively short-term food shortages could prompt precisely those social and political tensions which are the precursors of conflict. Marxist and isolated North Korea is the most frequently cited example of the potential impact of food shortages on regional security.

Televised images of North Korean peasants scouring the countryside for edible roots and grass to supplement their rations have increased in the 1990s. Some reports, including one attributed to a senior North Korean official, claim that 2.8m people have died from malnutrition since 1995.[31] However, the regime's obsessive

Figure 1 *North Korean Grain Supplies, 1991–1997*

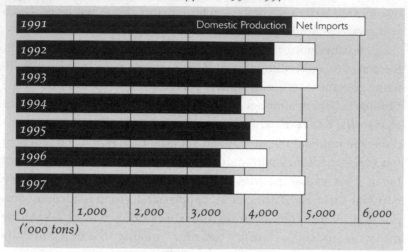

Source South Korean National Unification Board (NUB) estimates in Phillip
Wonhyuk Lim, 'North Korea's Food Crisis', *Korea and World
Affairs*, vol. 21, no. 4, Winter 1997, p. 582

secrecy and the lack of even rudimentary data on the population, economy and agriculture make it difficult to judge whether the country faces mass starvation. There are well-founded suspicions that Pyongyang has played upon the sympathies and fears of its neighbours and the wider international community to extract political concessions and food aid in a bid to strengthen its hold on power.

Nonetheless, most experts accept that food shortages in North Korea are severe and pose a major threat to the long-term survival of the regime. The state's food shortfall increased steadily throughout the 1990s, and was further compounded by adverse weather conditions in 1995–97.[32] The country recorded a grain shortfall of about one million tons in 1996, or half its projected needs, with the average diet down to a little over one bowl of rice a day.[33] A year later, North Koreans were subsisting on a daily ration of 100 grams of corn, one-fifth of the daily minimum requirement.[34] According to the UN's World Food Programme (WFP), many city-dwellers in North Korea receive only 15% of the daily ration given to refugees in Africa's camps.[35] Some 800,000 North Korean children are malnourished, 80,000 of them seriously.[36] The situation was unlikely to improve in

1998, when the UN Development Programme (UNDP) expected a food shortfall of up to three million tons.[37]

The seeds of North Korea's food problems were sown decades earlier, when the *juche* ('self-reliance') philosophy was first developed by 'Great Leader' Kim Il Sung. It is, however, doubtful whether North Korea could ever have become self-sufficient in staple foods given its generally inhospitable terrain and climate and relatively large population. Overshadowing this policy failure were a number of self-inflicted environmental disasters. Collectivisation was accompanied by large-scale land clearance and deforestation designed to expand the area available for cultivation. Once trees had been felled, rain washed away a large proportion of the replacement crops, causing soil erosion and serious flooding. The rate of deforestation accelerated as peasants felled trees for fuel, chemical fertilisers were over-used and soil fertility decreased. By the mid-1980s, exhausted soils had forced North Korea into dependence on food imports.

The security implications of North Korea's food scarcity extend beyond the stability or survival of the state. The country's natural and man-made environmental disasters have caused a sharp rise in the number of North Koreans crossing the border into the Yanbian region of China's Jilin province, where ethnic Koreans comprise about 40% of the local population.[38] China's desire to stem this flow is a principal factor in Beijing's decision to offer food assistance to Pyongyang. Likewise, South Korea's decision to provide food aid is stimulated by security as well as humanitarian considerations. After floods in September 1995, which uprooted large numbers of people and exacerbated North Korea's food shortages, South Korean officials moved quickly to establish refugee camps and a system for dealing with large influxes of North Koreans.[39]

North Korea should be seen as a salutary, but extreme, example of what can happen when man-made environmental degradation, adverse weather conditions and poor government policies combine to undermine a state's ability to provide for its citizens.

North Korea is a salutary, but extreme, example

Nonetheless, the country's difficulties illustrate several important general points about the links between food scarcity and security.

The first is that food shortages are generally symptomatic of flawed political and economic systems or policy failures. Second, while there is a direct link between environmental degradation and the region's declining agricultural productivity, the relationship between the environment and security is more tenuous: food shortages, although a contributing factor, are seldom a primary cause of conflict.

Fish Shortages

In 1990, the world's fish catch fell for the first time in 13 years.[40] Per capita fish availability declined by about 10% between 1990 and 1995, despite the $45bn-worth of annual subsidies governments give their fishing industries.[41] The UN estimates that another 16m tons of fish will be required by 2010. In response to rising demand, 136,000 new ships have been added to the world's fishing fleets since 1989, accelerating the decline in supply and causing prices to rise.[42] Between 1981 and 1991, the value of exports from the world's fisheries rose by 260%, from $15bn to $39bn.[43] In 1994, a World Bank study warned that 'the current harvesting capacity of the world's fleet far exceeds the estimated biological sustainability of most commercial species'.[44]

For an estimated one billion Asians, fish is the main source of protein and fishing supports more people than in any other region of the world. Over half the world's fish catch is taken in Asian waters, and five of the top ten fishing nations are in Pacific Asia.[45] For most states in the region, therefore, the relationship between food security, ecological damage and conflict is most evident at sea. In 1996, Rear-Admiral R. M. Sunardi, the senior adviser to Indonesia's Minister of Defence, described the Pacific as the region's 'rice bowl' for the twenty-first century.[46] However, the Pacific is showing signs of environmental degradation caused by coastal pollution, over-fishing and unsustainable exploitation of other forms of living marine resources.

The depletion of fish species is a major concern in the Northwest Pacific, which provides nearly one-third of the world's marine harvest.[47] Fish stocks in the Yellow, South and East China Seas have also fallen significantly in the 1990s.[48] While aqua-culture may meet some of the shortfall in supply, it is unlikely to become a substitute for marine fishing. Fish-farming requires far more resources than harvesting fish caught in the wild, and can cause significant environmental damage.[49]

Conflict over Fish

As traditional fishing-grounds are exhausted, competition for remaining stocks has intensified. In the late 1990s, countries which once welcomed foreign fishing fleets were restricting their access and quotas, while fishing nations had become much more protective of their own resources.[50] Japan, which relies heavily on fish as a dietary staple, was allowed to catch 1.2m tons' worth in the 200-mile US EEZ in 1981; by 1988, quotas had been cut virtually to zero.[51] South Korea and Taiwan have suffered similar reductions, and their trawlers have been forced well into the South Pacific to make up the shortfall. The fishing fleets of South-east Asia have also been compelled to move further afield, and the Chinese seem likely to join the hunt for dwindling stocks by building more ocean-going trawlers.[52]

As fishing fleets grow and venture further into the Pacific, the area of ocean open to international fishing is shrinking. A large percentage of the marine resources of the Western Pacific are either claimed or contested.[53] As a result, the frequency and seriousness of incidents at sea have steadily increased as foreign trawlers have illegally encroached into other countries' EEZs and territorial waters (see Map 3, page 52). Gun-battles have broken out between the Navies of regional states intent on defending the activities of national fishing fleets or preventing perceived territorial violations.

Fishing Disputes in South-east Asia

In South-east Asia, competition for fish and other living marine resources has historically been most intense in the Gulf of Thailand. With the third-largest fishing fleet in Pacific Asia, Thai fishermen had begun to exhaust stocks in their traditional fishing-grounds by the late 1970s and to encroach into the EEZs and territorial waters of neighbouring states.[54] In the 1980s and 1990s, seizures of Thai fishing vessels became more common throughout South-east Asian waters, particularly along the Tenasserim coast of Myanmar, the Gulf of Tonkin, the Luzon Strait and in the waters off Indonesia.

Illegal fishing by Thai vessels has been a worsening source of friction between Bangkok and its neighbours during the 1990s. In

Map 3 *Clashes over Fish in Pacific Asia, 1994–1997*

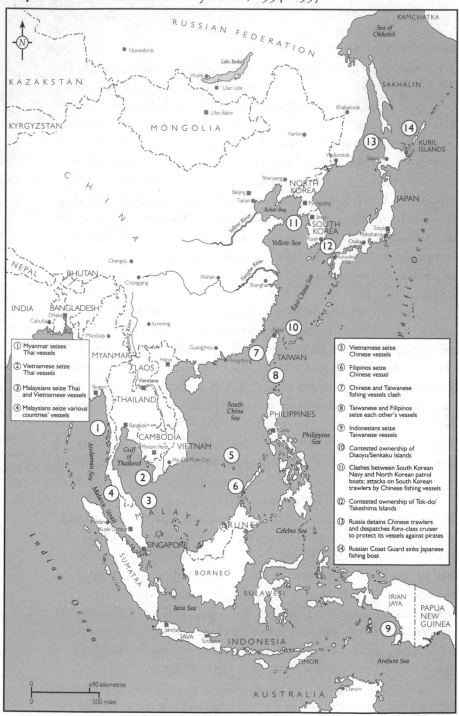

① Myanmar seizes Thai vessels

② Vietnamese seize Thai vessels

③ Malaysians seize Thai and Vietnamese vessels

④ Malaysians seize various countries' vessels

⑤ Vietnamese seize Chinese vessels

⑥ Filipinos seize Chinese vessel

⑦ Chinese and Taiwanese fishing vessels clash

⑧ Taiwanese and Filipinos seize each other's vessels

⑨ Indonesians seize Taiwanese vessels

⑩ Contested ownership of Diaoyu/Senkaku Islands

⑪ Clashes between South Korean Navy and North Korean patrol boats; attacks on South Korean trawlers by Chinese fishing vessels

⑫ Contested ownership of Tok-do/Takeshima Islands

⑬ Russia detains Chinese trawlers and despatches *Kara*-class cruiser to protect its vessels against pirates

⑭ Russian Coast Guard sinks Japanese fishing boat

the Andaman Sea, hundreds of Thai fishing vessels regularly plunder Myanmar's EEZ. Myanmar's Navy has minimal capability to protect the country's extensive coastline. The larger Thai vessels commonly carry heavy machineguns and rocket-propelled grenade launchers which they seldom hesitate to use if challenged. Thai fishermen also enjoy better intelligence information from radio centres that warn of approaching patrol boats.[55] Since 1995, Thai fishing vessels have also clashed with the Navies of Malaysia and Vietnam. On 31 May 1995, Thai and Vietnamese gunboats exchanged fire after the Thai Navy attempted to protect Thai fishing vessels from being seized by the Vietnamese Navy: a Thai fisherman and two Vietnamese sailors were killed and five of the six Thai fishing boats impounded, along with 62 of their crew.[56]

Thailand – which earned $3.4bn from fish exports in 1993 – may be the worst offender, but it is not the only culprit. The fishing vessels of virtually all South-east Asian states regularly intrude into neighbouring EEZs and territorial seas. Vietnam has fired on fishing boats from China, Malaysia and Taiwan, and the Philippines has seized Chinese and Taiwanese trawlers.[57] The arrest by the Philippines Navy of 23 Chinese fishermen on 12 August 1997 off the island of Palawan illustrates the potential of these disputes to damage broader political and security ties. China condemned the Philippines' action and warned that Manila ran the risk of ruining the 'friendly relations' between the two countries.[58]

States in the region have also enacted laws and established institutions to protect their marine resources from foreign poaching. In August 1997, the Indonesian government gave notice that it would ban foreign fishing vessels from its 6.5m km^2 of territorial waters from 2000.[59] In February 1997, the government inaugurated an 18-member National Maritime Council to 'protect the wealth and potential' of its seas against 'illegal exploitation by foreign parties'. Such 'exploitation' is estimated to cost Jakarta $1–2bn every year. In the Council's inauguration ceremony, Suharto made it clear that the protection of marine resources was closely linked with national security and defence.[60] On 6 August 1997, the Philippines Senate passed legislation imposing large fines on foreign poachers. Other states are expected to follow suit.[61]

Fish is central to the Spratlys dispute; according to one UN study, the waters around the Spratlys yield 7.5 tons of fish per square kilometre a year.[62] The abundance of commercially valuable tuna and shrimp has created lucrative fishing industries in virtually all the South China Sea littoral states, providing employment for millions of people as well as substantial foreign-exchange earnings. Malaysia, for example, earns about $50m a year from harvesting one species alone; the country puts the total value of tuna resources around the island of Layang-Layang in the Spratlys at around $600m.[63]

Fishing Disputes in North-east Asia

During the 1990s, illegal fishing, territorial/EEZ encroachments and maritime incidents in North-east Asia have become increasingly regular. The risk of significant political and military confrontation over competition for diminishing fish and other marine resources is emerging as a genuine security issue for China, Japan, the two Koreas and Russia.

There were 472 incidents of illegal fishing by Chinese ships in South Korea's 12-mile territorial waters in 1995.[64] In 1996, this figure rose by nearly 50%, prompting Seoul to place its Navy in the Yellow and Eastern Seas on alert. The move followed an attack by Chinese fishermen on a South Korean trawler in May in which 11 people were injured.[65] North Korean patrol boats have crossed into South Korean waters – violating the Military Demarcation Line – to protect their fishing fleet.[66] 'Fraternal relations' between the Chinese Communist Party and the North Korean Workers' Party did not prevent North Korean gunboats from firing on a fleet of Chinese trawlers in 1992. In 1994, Russia despatched a *Kara*-class cruiser to the East China Sea to halt what the Russian Foreign Ministry called 'pirate' attacks on its vessels. Russia has also detained Chinese trawlers for illegal fishing near the island of Sakhalin.[67]

Maritime incidents involving fish resources are linked to North-east Asia's most intractable territorial disputes. While most commentators have emphasised the geostrategic significance of the Diaoyu/Senkakus or the presence of oil as the underlying causes of the dispute over the islands, few seem to have recognised the importance of fish resources (Diaoyu Dao means 'fishing islands' in Chinese).[68] Taiwanese President Lee Teng Hui made clear in August 1996 that the real importance of the Diaoyu/Senkakus was related to fishing rights. Taiwan's national fishing association estimated in 1996 that the country's ships bring in about 40,000 tons of fish worth some $65m a year from the waters around the islands.[69]

In the North Pacific, the Kuril Island group is the subject of a long-running territorial dispute between Japan and Russia. The islands have important strategic and emotional significance for both countries because of the way in which they were 'acquired' by Moscow at the end of the Second World War. However, fish is also central to the dispute. The Kurils lie at the heart of one of the world's richest fishing grounds. Russia's ownership has allowed Moscow to claim an EEZ of 100,000km^2 containing fish, invertebrates and water-plants with an estimated market value of $1bn. Around 25% of Russia's annual fish catch of 6–7m tons comes from the southern Kuril region.[70]

Japan's determination to reclaim the Kurils has been reinforced by the knowledge that the region's rich marine resources would reduce the nation's dependence on more distant foreign waters. As the cost of deep-ocean fishing rises and other fish reserves near exhaustion, Japanese vessels seem increasingly prepared to risk penetrating the Russian EEZ around the Kurils. Since the end of the Cold War, the Russian Navy has seized numerous Japanese fishing boats. Tensions between the two states over fishing disputes increased in August 1994, when Moscow allowed its Border Guards to open fire on foreign vessels trespassing in Russian waters. A month later, the Russian Coast Guard sank a Japanese fishing boat.[71]

Until 1997, Japan had refrained from delineating fishing zones in the East China Sea and Sea of Japan to avoid aggravating historical disputes with China and South Korea over the Diaoyu/Senkaku and Tok-do/Takeshima islands. The government took this position despite intense pressure from the powerful domestic fishing industry, which had complained vociferously about Chinese and South Korean illegal fishing and attacks against Japanese fishing boats.[72] Tokyo has since, however, moved to tighten control over its own fishing grounds, while seeking to maximise access to the resources of disputed areas. In 1997, Tokyo declared a 200-nautical mile EEZ which incorporated the Tok-do/Takeshima group. South Korea, which has a small maritime-resource base, responded

swiftly by declaring its own 200-mile EEZ. South Korea's Foreign Minister Yoo Chong Ha stated that the zone 'starts from the limit of South Korea's territorial waters' and that Tok-do was 'within South Korean territorial waters'.[73]

Seoul's subsequent actions underline both the capacity of these disputes to escalate, and the increasing links between maritime food resources and territorial issues in post-Cold War Pacific Asia. Accusing Japan of violating the terms of a 1965 accord by unilaterally altering agreed fishing boundaries, Yoo Chong Ha demanded in July 1997 that Tokyo revoke its EEZ declaration until a new fishing agreement could be negotiated. The South Korean National Assembly passed a unanimous resolution protesting against Japan's 'illegal' change of the fishing boundaries.[74] Between 8 and 15 June 1997, the Japanese Maritime Safety Agency seized four South Korean fishing boats for allegedly penetrating the newly declared maritime boundary, further angering Seoul, which warned that such incidents would have grave consequences for the bilateral relationship.[75]Although the fishermen were eventually released, Japan refused to compromise on its boundary, and called instead on South Korea temporarily to recognise it and to give Japanese fishing fleets access to the waters around Tok-do.[76]

China and South Korea have also become embroiled in disputes over fish. Compared with the anger of South Korea's verbal attacks on Japan, fuelled in part by entrenched anti-Japanese animosity, Seoul had, until 1997, been relatively restrained in its response to Chinese illegal fishing. However, evidence of a much harder line emerged during talks in 1997 aimed at renegotiating fishing agreements to accommodate both countries' newly declared EEZs. The South Korean delegation urged China to crack down on illegal fishing in South Korean waters, and President Kim Young Sam's Cabinet banned foreign fishing vessels from entering designated prohibited zones in the West Sea from 7 November 1997.[77]

Inter-state confrontation over fish and other living resources is emerging as a significant long-term security problem. More generally, food is destined to have greater strategic weight and import in an era of environmental scarcity. While optimists maintain that the world is perfectly capable of meeting the anticipated increases in demand for essential foodstuffs, there are sufficient imponderables to suggest that prudent governments would not want to rely on such a felicitous outcome.

Food scarcity most commonly becomes a security issue as a result of sudden and unexpected fluctuations in supply and demand or, as in the extreme case of North Korea, of political and economic failure. Neither a sudden fluctuation, nor a failure on the North Korean scale, is likely in the immediate future, and Pacific Asia is unlikely to encounter insurmountable problems in feeding itself. Although tensions over diminishing fish supplies will increase, major food shortages are most likely to threaten the security of states when they coincide with other threats to *fishing disputes are a long-term security problem* political and economic stability. It can be argued that, as Pacific Asia battled in 1997–98 against the most serious financial and economic crisis in its modern history, these other threats were present. However, the real food-security issue for Pacific Asia in the long term is the cumulative and accelerating destruction of the region's food-producing capacity through a combination of population pressure and ecological degradation. For this reason, preserving arable land, protecting coastal and marine habitats and managing natural resources in a sustainable way may become intrinsic to conflict prevention.

chapter 5

Water Scarcity

Global Fresh Water Scarcity

Water is another environmental issue which has assumed a new prominence in the international security agenda of the 1990s. The link between fresh water and security is the result of water's central importance to human life and economic development. Water is arguably the most critical of all renewable resources because humankind depends upon continuous access to it, not only for drinking and food production, but also for industry, transport and energy. In the early 1990s, agriculture accounted for about 65%, and industry nearly 24%, of global water use.[1]

Between 1850 and 1993, per capita water supply fell by just under 75%, from 33,300 cubic metres to 8,500 cubic metres a year.[2] Population growth was primarily responsible for this decline. In late 1996, the FAO warned that 'human demands are about to collide with the ability of the hydrological cycle to supply water'.[3] The FAO warning was given added weight by a 1997 UN report which found that, by 2025, 'as much as two-thirds of the world's population could be under [water] stress conditions'. The report predicted that water shortages and pollution could place global food supplies in jeopardy, possibly leading to 'a series of local and regional water crises with global implications'.[4]

Three factors are responsible for the widening gap between demand for fresh water and its availability. First, the global supply of fresh water is limited and unevenly distributed. Fresh water constitutes less than 4% of the world's total water resources; most of that is locked away in glaciers and permanent snow cover, and only 0.007% is readily accessible for human use.[5] Second, water consumption has increased dramatically in the second half of the twentieth century. Global water use doubled between 1940 and 1980, and is expected to double again by 2000.[6] Irrigated land, which provides one-third of the world's harvest, has increased five-fold in area since 1900.[7] As a result, water has become a scarce resource in many parts of the world: some 80 countries containing 40% of the world's population suffer from serious shortages.[8] Per capita availability of good potable water is declining in developed states, as well as in developing ones.[9]

Finally, existing supplies of fresh water have been degraded and reduced by unsustainable environmental practices, especially in developing states. Over-logging and deforestation destroy water tables and cause silting and salinisation. Poor farming techniques prompt soil erosion, clogging waterways, and the overuse of pesticides and chemical fertilisers pollutes water used for drinking and irrigation. The expansion of urban areas, which are generally located near major river systems or in ecologically sensitive coastal areas, has further reduced fresh-water supplies.

Water Scarcity and Conflict

Does water scarcity necessarily lead to conflict? The historical record is ambiguous. The availability of fresh water has for centuries been a problem for the inhabitants of dry and desert regions, and has in many instances been aggravated by the frequently arbitrary political division of unitary river basins.[10] However, the number of cases in which water is an important or contributing cause of conflict in the arid Middle East appears to be increasing. There are currently disputes between Iraq, Syria and Turkey over the Euphrates River; Israel, Jordan, Lebanon and Syria over the headwaters of the Jordan River; and between the nine riparian Nile states.

Several prominent political leaders have publicly stated that nations will eventually go to war over water, including the former UN Secretary-General, Boutros Boutros-Ghali, who in the late 1980s predicted that the next war in the Middle East would be 'over the waters of the Nile, not politics'.[11] Some analysts argue that water might become more valuable than oil as a strategic resource and that water shortages in the Middle East will lead to 'unprecedented upheavals' between states.[12]

Emphasising the conflict potential of water shortages does not give the complete picture. Water-sharing arrangements are part of the political landscape of the Middle East, and conservation occupies an important place in the agendas of national governments. Technological advances, such as improved irrigation techniques and more effective water-distribution systems, demonstrate that, with sufficient political will, governments can considerably reduce wastage and increase the volume of usable water. Political difficulties arise when two or more states are forced to share surface and sub-surface water resources, as is the case with a great percentage of the Middle East's water. Even so, for all the warnings of impending 'water wars', at least one authoritative study has found that 'there is very little evidence so far of actual conflict in the Middle East directly and exclusively related to the control and exploitation of water resources'.[13]

Water Scarcity in Pacific Asia

To what extent is water scarcity likely to become a source of conflict in Pacific Asia? Judging by the frequency and severity of flooding during the region's wet season, tropical South-east Asia would seem to suffer from too much water, rather than too little. Pacific Asia is, however, beginning to encounter the quantitative and qualitative water limitations that other, drier parts of the world such as the Middle East have experienced for several decades. In Asia as a whole, per capita water availability has declined by between 40% and 65% since 1950 (see Table 7, below). According to the World

Table 7 *Annual Per Capita Water Availability by Region, 1950–2000*

('000 m³)	1950	1960	1970	1980	2000
Latin America	105	80.2	61.7	48.8	28.3
North America	37.2	30.2	25.2	21.3	17.5
Africa	20.6	16.5	12.7	9.4	5.1
Asia	9.6	7.9	6.1	5.1	3.3
Europe	5.9	5.4	4.9	4.4	4.1

Source FAO, *The State of Food and Agriculture, 1993*, www.fao.org

Bank, by 2025 most states in the region will be facing serious water shortages unless strong action is taken.[14]

This steep decline is the direct result of Pacific Asia's high population growth, the degradation of existing reserves of fresh water and the destruction of water tables through deforestation, urbanisation and environmentally insensitive agricultural methods. In North-east Asia, urban pollution is jeopardising water supplies in Japan, South Korea and Taiwan. Deforestation in particular is taking a heavy toll on the region's water quality. Tropical forests protect fragile soils from temperature and rainfall extremes. Removing trees usually triggers a cycle of flooding and drought that ends in substantial soil erosion and, in extreme cases, desertification.[15] Deforestation has seriously disrupted the water cycle in Cambodia, China, Indonesia, Laos, Myanmar, the Philippines and Thailand.[16] Nearly 50% of South-east Asia's forest cover has been destroyed. The FAO puts the annual rate of loss at around 1% (see Table 8, page 63); the World Bank estimates that some 1.4% of forest cover in the wider Pacific Asian region is being lost annually – a substantially higher rate of loss than in any other developing region.[17] Four main processes are responsible:

- 'slash and burn' agricultural practices;
- commercial timber extraction, both legal and illegal;
- government-sponsored transmigration schemes which accelerate the rate of deforestation in the remaining areas of virgin forest land; and
- large-scale development projects, such as mining operations and dam-building, which frequently require extensive forest clearance.[18]

In some states, Thailand for example, most of the commercially valuable tropical forest has already been cleared. In others, notably Cambodia, Laos and Myanmar, weak government controls and corruption have allowed loggers to fell large tracts of the oldest and most valuable timber.[19] In 1900, 70–80% of the Philippines was forested, compared with 20% by the mid-1990s. The Philippines imports more tropical timber than it produces; Malaysia is likely to do the same once remaining stands of old-growth forest are exhausted early in the twenty-first century.[20] China's extensive

Table 8 *Changes in Forest Cover in Pacific Asia, 1990–1995*

('000 ha)	1990	1995	Annual change
China	133,756	133,323	-0.1%
Indonesia	115,213	109,791	-1.0
Myanmar	29,088	27,151	-1.4
Japan	25,212	25,146	-0.1
Malaysia	17,472	15,471	-2.4
Thailand	13,277	11,630	-2.6
Laos	13,177	12,435	-1.2
Cambodia	10,649	9,830	-1.6
Vietnam	9,793	9,117	-1.4
Philippines	8,078	6,766	-3.5
South Korea	7,691	7,626	-0.2
North Korea	6,170	6,170	0
Brunei	448	434	-0.6
Singapore	4	4	0
Total	**390,028**	**374,894**	**-0.8**

Source   FAO, *The State of the World's Forests, 1996,* www.fao.org

reforestation campaign follows centuries of massive forest loss.[21] By one estimate, Indonesia allows up to 50% more logging than can be sustained.[22]

Thailand

In Thailand, unlicensed use of ground water from Bangkok's major aquifer is depleting ground-water supplies and causing the underground water table to fall by 2–4 metres a year. Pollution from untreated sewage and industrial waste is degrading Thailand's river systems and ground water.[23] The World Bank has warned the government that municipal authorities will not be able to guarantee drinking water to Bangkok's residents after 2025.

Bangkok's water shortages are also taking their toll on food production. The Chao Phraya river basin is critically important because it drains virtually all northern and central areas of the country and provides most of Thailand's agricultural produce. However, in 1993 the Bangkok Metropolitan Waterworks Authority informed Chao Phraya farmers that they would not be able to plant a second rice crop because Bangkok's need for additional water meant that supplies for agriculture were insufficient.[24]

Indonesia

After decades of environmental abuse, Indonesia is also beginning to suffer from recurrent water shortages. By 2005, Jakarta will consume six times as much water as it did in 1990; by 2025, an estimated 39m people will live in the greater Jakarta area, placing additional strains on fresh-water supplies.[25] Ground water is expected to provide 27% of the city's additional needs, but the water table is dropping and it is doubtful whether this target can be met. There are plans to draw additional supplies from rivers in West Java, but these are themselves under pressure from pollution and increased usage.[26] An associated problem is flooding caused by the destruction of the ecological system in the Jakarta area, especially the disappearance of the lakes and ponds that catch the overflow from monsoon rains.[27]

In the early 1990s, a World Bank study estimated that 1% of Jakarta's GDP was being spent on boiling water to make it fit for drinking.[28] In late 1995, Director-General of Water Resources Soeparmono warned that the situation was becoming dangerous.[29] Other cities in Java face comparable problems. The quality and quantity of water from the Brantas River system which supplies Surabaya, Indonesia's second-largest city, are falling rapidly because of unprecedented demand from a rising population and contamination due to urbanisation and industrial run-off.[30]

China

While China's overall population doubled between 1950 and 1990, its urban population quintupled and the area of irrigated land tripled. As a result, the national water deficit is expected to grow six-fold, from 15m tons a day in 1990 to 88m in 2000.[31] Beijing's chronic water shortages are typical: 300 cities in northern China suffer from similar problems, 50 of them severely so. In 1993, the Minister of Water Resources, Niu Mao Sheng, estimated that over 82m people in rural areas were finding it difficult to obtain water.[32]

Although in theory China has sufficient fresh-water resources to meet additional needs, its distribution throughout the country is highly uneven. Declining water quality, as well as quantity, is also a cause for concern:

- in the late 1980s, 82% of the country's 878 major rivers were polluted, more than 20% of them to the point where their water was useless for irrigation;
- at least four-fifths of China's surface water in urban areas is contaminated;
- in only six of China's 27 largest cities is the quality of drinking water within government safety limits. In August 1994, a senior Chinese official stated that 86% of the rivers flowing through the country's urban areas were seriously polluted;
- in coastal cities such as Tianjin, the ground-water level is dropping, allowing sea water to pollute underground reserves; and
- pollution has meant that the numbers of fish caught in fresh water have fallen significantly. In the Yangtse River, the catch of four major species was, in the mid-1990s, only 5% of 1970 levels.[33]

The Security Implications of Water Scarcity

The declining quality and per capita supply of fresh water is likely to impinge on the security of Pacific Asia in a number of ways. Continued decline will reduce the region's capacity to feed itself. The 'green revolution' was accomplished largely by increasing the area of land under irrigation and improving irrigation technology. By the early 1990s, global irrigated cropland produced one-third of the world's harvest, despite comprising just 17% of total cropland.[34] Asia has the greatest percentage of cropland under irrigation and depends on irrigated land for its food to a far greater extent than other regions. While irrigation accounts for over two-thirds of the fresh water used globally, in rice-dependent states such as China, 87% of water goes to agriculture.[35] It takes 5,000 kilograms of water to produce just one kilogram of rice.[36]

Conservation measures, alternative sources of fresh water and technological solutions such as water-desalinisation plants will partly alleviate water scarcity, but there is a limit to the extent to which these measures can provide a substitute for naturally occurring fresh water. In addition, Pacific Asia's poor track record raises doubts over regional governments' commitment to water conservation. In the longer term, however, failure to act will be costly: water shortages were estimated to cost the Chinese government between $620m and $1.06bn in 1990.[37]

Population displacement caused by the construction of dams and flood-control reservoirs may prompt political instability and violence within states. In the early 1970s, the Philippines decided to exploit the hydro-electric potential of northern Luzon by building a series of dams on the Chico River. Manila planned to clear large areas of land and to relocate 140,000 people. Local tribespeople resisted the project throughout the 1970s and early 1980s. At first, resistance took the form of peaceful protest but, after the area was militarised by President Ferdinand Marcos, the conflict became violent in 1976. The communist New People's Army (NPA) portrayed itself as the protector of the rights of the local tribespeople and, while the project did not create the NPA, it made local communities sympathetic to the group's anti-government struggle, thereby prolonging its insurgency.[38] By 1980, 100 people had been killed in fighting and the region had become ungovernable.[39] Six years later, the project was abandoned.

The Three Gorges scheme on China's Yangtse River is another example of the potential problems associated with water-related infrastructure projects. The scheme is officially – and conservatively – estimated to cost $25bn. It will transform the central portion of the Yangtse into the world's largest dam, creating a 632km^2 lake and generating 18,200 megawatts of electricity by 2009 – approximately the amount produced annually by 18 nuclear-power stations or 50m tons of coal. Apart from playing a major role in supplying China's future energy needs, the government expects the dam to control the Yangtse's periodic and disastrous floods.[40]

These are goals which would once have enjoyed considerable financial, political and popular support. The Three Gorges Dam has, however, been widely criticised. The World Bank has refused to provide financing; the project's critics warn that the lake behind the dam could become choked with sewage and industrial chemicals.[41] Many of the industrial sites which will be flooded by the scheme are saturated with hazardous waste (one, the Chongqing steel mill, was described by the World Bank in the early 1990s as among the ten most contaminated industrial sites in the world).[42] Scientists predict that the weight of the lake could trigger an earthquake, damaging the dam and threatening millions of people downstream. Environmental concerns coincide with objections against the damage that the dam will inflict on the culturally and historically significant land it will submerge.

Opposition to the Three Gorges project demonstrates the increasingly politicised nature of large-scale infrastructure development. Environmental opposition to large development projects represents a new factor that regional governments will need to take into account when formulating policy, but its security implications will be low-key. Regional governments should be able to manage opposition without recourse to violence.

The Inter-state Dimension

Water scarcity is likely to assume broader and more serious security ramifications when it becomes entangled with other sources of tension between states. Water security is a key strategic issue for Singapore. Because of its small size, relatively flat terrain and high population density, Singapore has never been self-sufficient in water, and relies on piped supplies from Malaysia to meet just under 50% of its needs. In 1997, Singapore piped around 1.5bn litres of untreated water from Malaysia, of which 150m litres were sold back in treated form.

In 1961 and 1962, Singapore signed two water-sharing agreements with Kuala Lumpur. Under the 1961 agreement, which expires in 2011, Singapore's Public Utilities Board (PUB) is entitled to draw unlimited water from the Tebrau and Scudai Rivers and the Pontian and Gunong Pulai catchment areas in Malaysia's Johor state. The 1962 agreement, which expires in 2061, allows the PUB to draw up to 1.12bn litres of water a day from the Johor River. Neither country can unilaterally abrogate these arrangements under the terms of the 'Separation Agreement', signed on 9 August 1965, which ended Singapore's affiliations with Malaysia.[43]

Since half of Singapore's land area is used as water catchment, improved conservation and a pricing scheme that more accurately reflects the actual cost of water will offer little scope for increasing domestic supplies. In addition to negotiating a water-sharing agreement with Indonesia's Riau province, Singapore is examining desalinisation technology and is expected to have an operational desalinisation plant by 2003.[44] These plants are expensive – about $1bn each – and can produce only around 135m litres of water a year,

water security matters to Singapore

less than one-third of Singapore's domestic shortfall.[45] Singapore will therefore remain dependent on Malaysian water for the foreseeable future. The water relationship between the two states is complicated by Malaysia's own impending water-supply problems. Two of the country's most populous states, Negri Sembilan and Selangor – which includes Kuala Lumpur – are expected to exhaust their water supplies by 2000, with some Malaysian experts predicting that shortages will reach crisis-point in 2010.[46]

Singapore's relations with Malaysia have historically been clouded by disagreements stemming from economic competition and political, religious and ethnic differences. These disputes have flared periodically since 1965. In 1997, a public row between the two states followed comments by Singapore's former Prime Minister, Lee Kuan Yew, that Johor state was 'notorious for shootings, muggings and car-jackings'.[47] Public and press reaction in Malaysia was overwhelmingly critical, and Ahmed Zamid Hamidi, the head of the Youth Wing of Malaysia's ruling party, the United Malays National Organisation (UMNO), urged the government to review the basis of water and air-space agreements with Singapore.[48] Johor Chief Minister Abdul Ghani suggested that Johor should consider taking over two of the three water-purification plants on its soil operated by Singapore.[49] In an unusually frank disclosure to his parliament in June 1997, Singapore's Prime Minister, Goh Chok Tong, recounted that he had raised the water issue with his Malaysian counterpart, Mahathir Mohamad, at the inaugural Asia–Europe Meeting in Bangkok on 2 March 1996, and had argued that 'an agreement by Malaysia to meet Singapore's long-term water needs beyond the life of the present water agreements would remove the perception in Singapore that water may be used as a leverage [sic] against Singapore'.[50] Tensions later eased, although, when announcing price increases for water in June 1997, Singapore's Deputy Prime Minister,

Lee Hsien Loong, directly linked the rises to the earlier Malaysian threats. 'You have seen how water is an item that can be used to pressure us', he commented:

> *The bottom line is: Water is a strategic resource ... It's not like air, which you can have for free. It's not like fuel for buses or cars which you can always import any amount of ... it is something which is limited. When you run out you are up against, if not a brick wall, at least a very, very steep slope.*[51]

The Mekong River Basin

Competition for water might also emerge as a source of conflict among the six riparian states of the Mekong River basin in mainland South-east Asia. At 4,200km in length, the Mekong is the largest river system in South-east Asia and the only major river in Pacific Asia which flows through more than two sovereign states.[52]

Economic and population growth in the greater Mekong region has significantly increased the value and importance of the river's waters. The Mekong sustains the world's largest fresh-water lake, the Tonle Sap, which is vital to Cambodia for fish, irrigation and transport. The seven Cambodian provinces abutting the lake account for 40% of the country's annual rice production of 2.4m tons, and are home to four million of the nation's nine million people.[53] Vietnam is arguably the most dependent of all the Mekong states on the river's resources. The rich flood-plain of the Mekong Delta provides more than half of the country's rice, a substantial portion of which is exported, while some 15m Vietnamese rely on the Mekong for fish.[54] Thailand uses the river's waters to irrigate its arid north-eastern provinces, and plans to harness them for hydro-electric power. Mountainous Laos, the smallest and poorest of the states along the Mekong, sees the river as its economic salvation: 40% of the rivers feeding into the Mekong originate in the mountains and highlands of Laos, and Vientiane has developed ambitious plans to build hydro-electric dams on its portion of the river to provide energy for Thailand and Vietnam. China is also beginning to tap the river's hydro-electric potential. The first dam across the Mekong, in China's Yunnan province, began generating electricity in 1993. China plans to build

Map 4 *The Mekong River Basin*

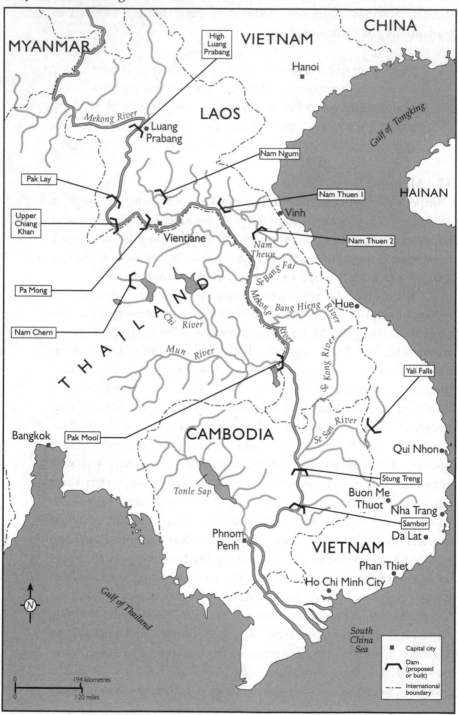

a further 14 dams in Yunnan alone, five on the Mekong itself and nine on its tributaries. These will produce 20,000 megawatts of power, more than the capacity of the Three Gorges Dam. Altogether, some 54 dams are planned or are under way along the length of the Mekong and its tributaries.[55]

The idea of bringing together the states along the lower reaches of the Mekong to control the waters for their mutual benefit was first mooted in the 1950s. The UN established a Mekong Committee in 1957, but successive wars in Indochina prevented significant progress.[56] Negotiations resumed in the early 1990s and, in April 1995, Cambodia, Laos, Thailand and Vietnam signed a historic accord designed to improve the management of the river's waters

the flawed agreement could lead to problems

under the auspices of the Mekong River Commission. Known as the 'Agreement on Cooperation for the Sustainable Development of the Mekong River Basin', the accord allows its members freedom of navigation along the river and establishes a water-sharing regime. The agreement was hailed as a breakthrough in cooperation between states which, only two decades before, were at war.

However, the agreement also contains the seeds of potential future conflict over the Mekong's resources. A key provision allows each state to divert the river's waters without seeking the approval of other members, except during the dry season.[57] This so-called 'no-veto rule' contradicts a 1957 agreement requiring detailed studies by all parties before implementing projects which might affect the flow of the Mekong or its tributaries. Since they are not obliged to secure other states' approval for projects, signatory countries may be tempted to place their short-term interests ahead of the welfare of the river and of the wider sub-region. Only eight of the 54 Mekong dams envisaged or in operation have been subject to environmental-impact studies, and there has been no serious attempt to assess the overall effect of the dams on the Mekong's flow.[58] The minority hill-tribes most likely to be affected have been largely ignored in the rush to harness the Mekong's resources. These tribal people have a history of militant opposition to central government control in China, Laos, Myanmar and Thailand. China's refusal to sign the 1995 accord also raises doubts about the effectiveness of a co-operative agreement which fails to include the country with the greatest capacity to control the river's flow. China insists that whatever action it takes to exploit the Mekong's potential is purely an internal matter.

The extensive soil loss, deforestation and land degradation in the Mekong basin, together with the construction and operation of the dams, will upset the river's ecological balance. Forest cover along the basin declined from about 50% of the land area to some 27% in 1970–85. As new hydro-electric dams are built, and the Mekong basin develops, the rate of deforestation will accelerate.[59] The ambitious hydro-electric plans of China and Laos will substantially reduce the level of the river's seasonal flooding. One reservoir planned by the Chinese is of particular concern because it could hold the entire flow of the upper Mekong for up to six months.[60] A scientific study carried out on the environmental effects of damming the Mekong has found that the reduction in water volume will eventually clog its mouth. The river's salinity will also increase and its rich deposits of silt, vital for regenerating the surrounding agricultural land, will disappear. Interrupting the natural cycle of the Mekong could be fatal for the fresh-water fishing industries of Cambodia and Vietnam. It could also seriously diminish the 'carrying capacity' of the land which provides 40% of Vietnam's agricultural output.[61]

Perennially dry areas of the world such as the Middle East are accustomed to living without an excess of water. However, water scarcity is a relatively new experience for Pacific Asian states and a looming resource problem. Regional governments are ill-equipped – psychologically and in policy terms – to deal with it. Second, Pacific Asia's water supply and demand are subject to much greater fluctuations than those of the Middle East because of demographic factors and wide seasonal variations in rainfall. If the wet season is late, or fails altogether, water supplies may fall quickly and sharply. Finally, when Pacific Asia's populations were much smaller and dispersed, water shortages tended to be relatively short term, localised and far more manageable than the man-made, systemic shortages now confronting the region.

As with other scarce resources, conflict will not necessarily follow from the declining availability of fresh water in Pacific Asia. The underlying strength of the political relationship between states sharing water resources is crucial in determining whether disputes escalate. Countries with shared values and generally cooperative relations are less likely to go to war over water than those with a history of enmity and confrontation. It is difficult to see nations in Pacific Asia going to war over water in the manner that some have predicted in the Middle East. Water scarcity will, however, affect the region's security environment in two principal ways.

Domestically, water shortages will aggravate social and political tensions, complicating the internal security challenges faced by the region's developing states. Internationally, the importance of water as one of the factors prompting inter-state conflict will increase. As economic and political inter-dependence grows, the water problems of one state will become the concern of all. This is especially the case in South-east Asia, raising the prospect that ASEAN may feel obliged to assist in adjudicating or resolving water disputes between its members. These disputes are most likely to originate in the intensifying sub-regional competition for the resources of the Mekong River, which could become a catalyst for the re-emergence of historical grievances between the six riparian states. Maritime South-east Asian states share no land or river borders, and so seem less likely to become involved in conflicts over water. However, as the tensions between Malaysia and Singapore demonstrate, disputes over water resources may not be confined to the ownership of underground aquifers or river systems.

There can be no simple judgements about the impact of environmental issues on security in Pacific Asia. Those who see a close connection between environmental degradation and military conflict exaggerate their case: there is no compelling evidence that environmental problems have been the primary cause of any major sub-national or inter-state conflict. This is not, however, an argument for complacency. Ecological pressures will be increasingly important in shaping the economic and political environment in Pacific Asia and, by extension, its security environment. War is unlikely to result purely – or even primarily – for environmental reasons, but Pacific Asia suffers from many tensions that have environmental sources. Understanding security in Pacific Asia therefore requires an understanding of environmental issues.

The Environment and Security

In Pacific Asia, the influence of domestic environmental movements on policy-making has been relatively minor. Compared with Europe and North America, local environmentally focused non-governmental organisations (NGOs) in the authoritarian states of Pacific Asia have limited budgets and minimal support among political élites. Their activities are often seen as unpatriotic and as threatening the stability of regimes. In the more democratically vibrant states such as the Philippines, NGOs generally wield more influence, although there are notable exceptions.[1] In Japan, public awareness of environmental issues, though growing, remains unusually low, even by Asian standards.[2]

International NGOs concerned with the environment frequently enjoy more influence in Pacific Asia than their local counterparts because of their capacity to mobilise the Western media and their greater resources. The emergence of the environment as a major global issue has helped NGOs to influence government policy.[3] In a small minority of cases, extremists have used violence to challenge the authority of the state. In Pacific Asia, Malaysia, for example, has experienced logging blockades and sabotage by environmentalists intended to prevent environmental damage.[4]

Which environmental issues should gain most attention in the future? While pollution will have serious consequences for Pacific Asia's health and economic development, it is a second-order security issue because it will seldom be a leading cause of conflict. Nonetheless, air and sea pollution will occasionally assume greater political prominence when major oil spills and forest fires increase tensions between states and call into question the priorities and competence of governments. As in the case of the Indonesian fires, pollution can help to reshape the political agenda, and hence the overall security-policy climate, in significant ways.

Population growth has had a more palpable effect on regional security. Increases on the scale that Pacific Asia will experience in the twenty-first century will aggravate political and social divisions within states and accelerate the decline in the region's stocks of natural resources. The ability of China and Indonesia to manage effectively their projected population growth will be critical in determining regional stability. Demographic pressures on the environment are set to reduce the carrying capacity of the land in Pacific Asia's two most populous states, and will be most severely felt in and near major cities. Other regional states will have to deal with their own population problems as well as considering the transnational security implications of population growth in China and Indonesia.

Unless action is taken, water scarcity may become a major security issue for Pacific Asia. The extent of the problem will vary significantly within and between states. China, Indonesia, Singapore and Thailand suffer endemic water shortages and others may soon be affected. Long-term trends in use and supply point towards an accelerating deterioration in the region's reserves of fresh water. There is little prospect of reversing the trend without substantial and meaningful regional cooperation. Water disputes in South-east Asia have the capacity to exacerbate tensions between Malaysia and Singapore, and eventually to reawaken traditional animosities between the riparian states of the Mekong River. In the main, however, conflict over water is likely to be only one of several important challenges to domestic stability and governance. In the longer term, the declining availability of fresh water will indirectly affect regional security because of irrigation's critical role in rice-growing and hydro-electricity production.

Like the putative US–Soviet 'missile gap' of the 1960s, fears of an imminent and serious energy or food deficit in Pacific Asia may prove unfounded. Should serious shortfalls develop, Pacific Asia could trade its way out of a short-term crisis as other regions have done in the past. Aside from fish, there has been no sustained rise in global energy or food prices that would warn of a fundamental imbalance in supply and demand sufficiently grave to pose a major threat to the security interests of Pacific Asian states.

Environmental factors interact with other, more traditional, security issues; their impact and weight will vary and, in some cases, they may play no role at all.[5] The maritime disputes in the South and East China Seas illustrate well how this interweaving of traditional security concerns and environmental issues can drive conflict. Resource hunger has complicated the sovereignty issues at stake in these disputes. Without the pressure of rising populations, high levels of energy dependency and the exhaustion of fish and other marine living resources, the maritime-sovereignty issues in the Western Pacific would almost certainly not have attracted the same degree of prominence, nor proved as difficult to resolve.[6]

The Prospects for Cooperation

The governments of Pacific Asia have begun to explore the potential for environmental cooperation. At the national level, greater efforts are being made to correct some of the excesses of the past. Indonesia's Environmental Impact Management Agency (BAPEDAL), for example, has begun to evaluate the environmental record of private companies and to give a 'black rating' to the most serious offenders. Environmental officials in China closed down 50,000 polluting factories in 1996.[7]

In South-east Asia, the ASEAN Environmental Programme (ASEP) was established in 1978 to promote sustainable economic development and, in 1981, ASEAN issued its first major declaration on the environment. This was followed in 1990 by the Kuala Lumpur Accord on the Environment and Develop-

the early stages of environmental cooperation

ment that confirmed the commitment to sustainable economic development.[8] ASEAN has also taken initiatives to combat major oil spills by setting up the ASEAN Oil Spill Response and Preparedness (ASEAN-OSRAP) project.[9]

North-east Asia's track record on environmental cooperation has been less impressive. Nonetheless, environmental regimes are in place. These include the Northwest Action Plan, the Prevention and Management of Marine Pollution in the East Asia Seas and the Interim Scientific Committee for Tuna and Tuna-like Species (ISC), which held its first meeting in May 1996.[10] The Asia-Pacific Economic Cooperation (APEC) forum has also implemented region-wide environmental programmes. In July 1990, APEC began a dialogue on the maritime transport of hazardous substances, the discharge of marine pollutants and the problem of marine debris. In March 1994, the first conference of APEC Environment Ministers was held. A subsequent meeting in June 1997 approved an environmental action programme in the three priority areas of sustainable cities, a clean Pacific and clean production technologies.[11] The 'second-track' Council for Security Cooperation in the Asia-Pacific has devoted considerable attention to the security aspects of the environment, and has considered proposals aimed at safeguarding the marine environment and providing for 'environmentally responsible defence'.[12]

Despite these advances, the measures so far adopted by regional states to combat environmental degradation fall far short of what is required.[13] Most efforts have targeted the economic and maritime aspects of the problem which, although important, represent only part of the environmental picture.[14] What might

Pacific Asia's governments do to address the security implications of environmental degradation and resource depletion?

- At the national level, few states in Pacific Asia have integrated the environment into national-security planning.[15] An essential first step, therefore, is to increase awareness among policy-makers of the causal links between the environment and conflict. This will require considerably more focused and policy-oriented research of the issues identified in this paper.

- Second, it is clear that many environmental-security issues transcend state jurisdictions and are not amenable to national solutions. Pacific Asian governments must cooperate more closely in finding solutions to problems that concern them all. Despite the measures already adopted, the rhetorical commitment to dealing with the causes of ecological stress has yet to be backed up by effective programmes.

No multilateral organisation has assumed the task of formulating, prioritising and implementing an overarching strategy for analysing and managing environmental challenges to regional security. Rather than establish new bodies to assist national governments in this task, better use could be made of existing organisations. The ASEAN Regional Forum (ARF), the region's pre-eminent multilateral security body, would seem the appropriate organisation to take on these important and neglected tasks. Unless steps such as these are taken, regional efforts to grapple with the security dimension of resource scarcity and environmental degradation are likely to remain piecemeal, ill-directed and largely ineffective.

notes

Introduction

[1] See Barry Buzan, *People, States and Fear: An Agenda for International Security Studies in the Post-Cold War Era* (Hemel Hempstead: Harvester Wheatsheaf, 1991), especially p. 131; Jennifer Tuchman-Mathews, 'Redefining Security', *Foreign Affairs*, vol. 8, no. 1, Summer 1993, pp. 162–77; and Thomas Homer-Dixon, 'Environmental Scarcities and Violent Conflict: Evidence from Cases', *International Security*, vol. 19, no. 1, Summer 1994, p. 8.

[2] Daniel Deudney, 'The Case Against Linking Environmental Degradation and National Security', *Millennium: Journal of International Studies*, vol. 19, no. 1, 1990, pp. 461–64.

[3] For definitions of the term 'environmental security', see Buzan, *People, States and Fear*, particularly pp. 16–17, which summarise earlier attempts to define national security, and pp. 131–34; Richard Ullman, 'Redefining Security', *International Security*, vol. 8, no. 1, Summer 1993, p. 133; R. T. Maddock,

'Environmental Security in East Asia', *Contemporary Southeast Asia*, vol. 17, no. 1, June 1995, p. 20; Tuchman-Mathews, 'Redefining Security', p. 162; Mark Levy, 'Is the Environment a National Security Issue?', *International Security*, vol. 20, no. 2, Autumn 1995, pp. 37–41; and Stephen Libiszewski, 'What is an Environmental Conflict?', *Occasional Paper No. 1*, Environment and Conflicts Project, Swiss Peace Foundation, Bern, 1992, p. 3.

[4] See Franklyn Griffiths, 'Environment in the US Security Debate: The Case of the Missing Arctic Waters', *Environmental Change And Security Project Report*, Issue No. 3, The Woodrow Wilson Center, Spring 1997, pp. 18–19.

[5] See Robert K. Ackerman, 'Defence Machinery Gears up to Fight Environmental Threat', *Signal*, vol. 45, no. 4, December 1990, pp. 35–38; and Nathan Ruff, Robert Chamberlain and Alexandra Cousteau, 'Report on Applying Military and Security

Assets to Environmental Problems', *Environmental Change And Security Project Report*, Issue No. 3, p. 83.

[6] See, for example, Arthur Westing, 'Environmental Warfare: An Overview', in Westing (ed.), *Environmental Warfare: A Technical, Legal and Policy Appraisal* (London: Taylor and Francis, 1984), pp. 3–12; and Arthur Westing, 'Environmental Warfare: Manipulating the Environment for Hostile Purposes', paper presented at the Woodrow Wilson Center, Washington DC, 7 May 1996.

[7] This is a modified form of the definition given in Thomas Homer-Dixon, 'On the Threshold: Environmental Changes as Causes of Acute Conflict', *International Security*, vol. 16, no. 2, Autumn 1991, p. 77.

[8] *Ibid.*, p. 83; Levy, 'Is the Environment a National Security Issue?', pp. 56–57.

[9] Homer-Dixon, 'On the Threshold', p. 78.

[10] All but one of the world's major armed conflicts in 1996 were internal, rather than between states. Margareta Sollenberg and Peter Wallensteen, 'Major Armed Conflicts', in *SIPRI Yearbook 1997: Armaments, Disarmament and International Security* (Oxford: Oxford University Press for the Stockholm International Peace Research Institute (SIPRI), 1997), p. 19.

Chapter 1

[1] John McBeth, 'El Nino Gets Blamed', *Far Eastern Economic Review*, 9 October 1997, p. 80.

[2] Greg Earl, 'Neighbours Angry about "This Arson Thing"', *The Australian Financial Review*, 30 September 1994, p. 22.

[3] Derwin Pereira, 'Jakarta Spells Out More Measures to Halt Fires in Sumatra, Kalimantan', *The Sunday Times* (Malaysia), 14 September 1997, p. 1.

[4] 'The Haze Worsens', *The Straits Times*, 15 September 1997, p. 1.

[5] 'Where There's Smoke There's Serious, Long-term Damage', *The Australian*, 6 October 1997, p. 7.

[6] Murray Hiebert, S. Jayasankaran and John McBeth, 'Fire in the Sky', *Far Eastern Economic Review*, 9 October 1997, pp. 74–78.

[7] Of this $1.4 billion, Indonesia was estimated to have lost $1bn, Malaysia $300 million and Singapore $60m. These figures are from a 1998 World Wildlife Fund study. See Nick Edwards, 'More Smog May Wreck $40b Asian Tourism', *The Canberra Times*, 23 March 1998, p. 5; and Margot Cohen, Ben Dolven and Murray Hiebert, 'Yet Again', *Far Eastern Economic Review*, 19 March 1998, p. 22.

[8] See 'Indonesian Fires Could Cost US$6 Billion, Experts Say', *The Jakarta Post*, 18 March 1998, p. 1.

[9] Patrick Walters, 'When an Archipelago isn't an Island Entire of Itself', *The Australian*, 9 October 1997, p. 13.

[10] Patrick Walters, 'Indonesians Blame Killer Smoke Haze on Weather', *The Australian*, 29 September 1997, p. 6.

[11] Michael Richardson, 'Haze Battle a Litmus Test for ASEAN Ties', *The Australian*, 7 October 1997, p. 8.

[12] 'Forest Fires an Act of Environmental Terrorism', *The Nation*, 29 September 1997, p. A4.

[13] Richardson, 'Haze Battle a

Litmus Test for ASEAN Ties'.
[14] Louise Williams and Mark Baker, 'South-east Asia's Year of Reckoning', *The Sydney Morning Herald*, 6 October 1997, p. 9.
[15] Gautam Kaji, 'Challenges to the East Asian Environment', *The Pacific Review*, vol. 7, no. 2, 1994, p. 211.
[16] Williams and Baker, 'South-east Asia's Year of Reckoning'.
[17] By one estimate, the number of cars in East Asia is doubling every seven years. Kaji, 'Challenges to the East Asian Environment', p. 211.
[18] See, for example, S. Jayasankaran, 'Air of Concern', *Far Eastern Economic Review*, 17 November 1994, p. 50. Several national and international reports have urged remedial action. In 1993, a Malaysian Department of Environment study found that 73% of rivers surveyed in Peninsular Malaysia were 'biologically dead' or 'dying'; also in 1993, the Japanese International Cooperation Agency (JICA) reported that Kuala Lumpur's air quality would worsen significantly by 2005.
[19] Cited in Maddock, 'Environmental Security in East Asia', p. 29. The original calculations were made by Czech economist Vaclav Smil in 'Environmental Change as a Source of Conflict and Economic Losses in China', *Occasional Paper No. 2*, Project on Environmental Change and Acute Conflict, December 1992.
[20] Nick Edwards, 'Huge Clean-up Bill on the Way', *The Sydney Morning Herald*, 24 November 1997, p. 13.
[21] Douglas Murray, 'American Interests in China's Environment', *The Pacific Review*, vol. 7, no. 2, 1994, p. 218.
[22] Foreign Broadcast Information Service (FBIS), *Daily Report*, EAS-96-114, 12 June 1996, p. 48.
[23] Robert E. Bedeski, 'Unconventional Security and the Republic of Korea: A Preliminary Assessment', *CANCAPS Paper No. 8*, August 1995, p. 9; Murray, 'American Interests in China's Environment', p. 216.
[24] Maddock, 'Environmental Security in East Asia', p. 27.
[25] See Murray, 'American Interests in China's Environment', p. 216.
[26] Kari Huus, 'A Question of Economy', *Far Eastern Economic Review*, 17 November 1996, p. 52.
[27] Kevin Sullivan, 'Japanese Incinerator Fouls Navy Base's Air', *The Washington Post*, 24 November 1997, p. A18.
[28] See Julian Cribb, 'Toxic Red Tides Choke Asia's Seas', *The Weekend Australian*, 12–13 August 1995, p. 19.
[29] Vaclav Smil, 'Environmental Problems in China: Estimates of Economic Costs', *East–West Center Special Report No. 5*, April 1996, p. 28.
[30] Bedeski, 'Unconventional Security and the Republic of Korea', p. 10.
[31] Cited in Mark Valencia, 'Energy and Insecurity in Asia', *Survival*, vol. 39, no. 3, Autumn 1997, p. 101.
[32] Chris Betros, 'Evasion over Russian Tanker Angers Tokyo', *South China Morning Post*, 22 February 1997, p. 12.
[33] See 'Drifting Oil Tanker Threatens Spill in Malacca Strait', *The Canberra Times*, 22 January 1993, p. 11. On the growing incidence of marine pollution in South-east Asia, see Joseph

Morgan, 'Natural and Human Hazards', in Harold Brookfield and Yvonne Byron (eds), *Southeast Asia's Environmental Future: The Search for Sustainability* (Kuala Lumpur: Oxford University Press, 1993), p. 293.

[34] John H. Noer, 'Southeast Asian Chokepoints: Keeping Sea Lines of Communication Open', *Strategic Forum*, no. 98, December 1996, p. 3.

[35] See, for example, Hamidah Atan, Vincent De Paul and Azman Ahmad, 'Order to Detain Ship Served on Captain', *New Straits Times*, 2 June 1995, pp. 1–2.

[36] 'ASEAN Pools Fire-fighting Efforts', *The Australian*, 6 April 1998, p. 8.

Chapter 2

[1] Neville Brown, 'Climate, Ecology and International Security', *Survival*, vol. 31, no. 6, November–December 1989, p. 121.

[2] Unless otherwise indicated, the statistics in this analysis are taken from: *World Population Prospects: The 1996 Revision* (New York: United Nations, forthcoming), Annexes 1, 2 and 3; *Population Newsletter*, no. 62, Department for Economic and Social Information and Policy Analysis, UN Secretariat, December 1996, pp. 1–3; and *World Population Projections to 2050* (New York: Population Division, Department of Economic and Social Affairs, UN Secretariat, 1998), Executive Summary, pp. 1–2.

[3] Robert Engelman, 'Human Population Prospects: Implications for Environmental Security', *Environmental Change and Security Project Report*, pp. 48–49 and 51;

World Resources 1994–95: A Guide to the Global Environment (Oxford: Oxford University Press for the UN, 1994), p. 27; private discussions with Australian demographers.

[4] See, for example, Nicholas Eberstadt, 'Research: Too Few People', *Prospect*, no. 25, December 1997, p. 51.

[5] *Concise Report on the World Population Situation in 1993* (New York: UN, 1994), p. 14.

[6] See, for example, Ron Duncan, 'Long-term Income, Population and Food Interrelationships in the Asia-Pacific Region', paper presented at the 1997 Conference of the Australian College of Defence and Strategic Studies, Canberra, December 1997, especially pp. 1–11.

[7] *Concise Report on the World Population Situation in 1993*, p. 32; *Asia 1997 Yearbook* (Hong Kong: Far Eastern Economic Review, 1996), p. 69; Rahul Singh, 'Food for Thought: Too Many People Can Hamper Development', *Far Eastern Economic Review*, 22 September 1996, p. 26.

[8] Rahul Singh, 'Growing Pains: Cairo Conference Debates World's Demographic Future', *ibid.*, 22 September 1994, p. 20; Engelman, 'Human Population Prospects', p. 53.

[9] See Alan Dupont, 'Unregulated Population Flows in East Asia: A New Security Dilemma?', *Pacifica Review*, vol. 9, no. 1, May–June 1997, pp. 1–22.

[10] *World Population Prospects: The 1992 Revision* (New York: UN, 1993), Table A.12.

[11] *Concise Report on the World Population Situation in 1993*, pp. 12–13.

[12] *Ibid.*, p. 34.

[13] William McGurn, 'City Limits',

Far Eastern Economic Review, 6
February 1997, pp. 34–37; World
Bank discussion paper prepared
by Clive Bardon and Ramesh
Ramankutty cited in Florence
Chong, 'Asia's Economies May
Cost the Earth', *The Australian*, 30
March 1994, p. 39.
[14] Asian Development Bank (ADB)
figures cited in Johanna Son,
'Megacosts Keep Megacities
Unhealthy', *The Jakarta Post*, 23
April 1997, p. 5.
[15] J. Song and J. Y. Yu, 'The
Stability of Population and
Population Control Policies', in
Hermann Schbenell (ed.),
*Population Policies in Asian
Countries* (Hong Kong: Drager
Foundation and Center of Asian
Studies, 1984), p. 517.
[16] Lester Brown, *Who Will Feed
China?: Wake-up Call for a Small
Planet* (London: Earthscan
Publications, 1995), pp. 35–36.
[17] *Ibid.*, pp. 40–41.
[18] Greg Austin, 'The Strategic
Implications of China's Public
Order Crisis', *Survival*, vol. 27, no.
2, Summer 1995, pp. 7–23.
[19] See Phil Williams, 'The
Geopolitics of Transnational
Organized Crime', paper
presented at the seminar 'Global
Security Beyond 2000: Global
Population Growth,
Environmental Degradation,
Migration, and Transnational
Crime', University of Pittsburgh,
Pittsburgh, PA, 2–3 November
1995, p. 8.
[20] Yoshiko Matsushita, 'Japan
Fights Immigrant Wave', *Asia
Times*, 25 April 1997, p. 2.
[21] Cited in Alan Burnett, *The
Western Pacific: Challenge of
Sustainable Growth* (London: Allen
and Unwin, 1993), p. 77.
[22] World Bank projections cited in
'Expanding Horizons: Australia
and Indonesia into the 21st
Century', East Asia Analytical
Unit, Department of Foreign
Affairs and Trade, Canberra, 1994,
p. 23.
[23] See Deny Hidayati,
'Transmigration Settlement:
Development or Destruction?',
The Business Times (Singapore),
25–26 January 1997, p. 4.
[24] 'Problems Along Indonesia's
Border With Papua New Guinea
Continue', *Asian Defence Journal*,
February 1996, p. 114.
[25] PT Freeport operates the
world's largest copper and gold
mine at Tembagapura, Irian Jaya.
John McBeth, 'Army Under Fire',
Far Eastern Economic Review, 14
September 1995, p. 31; Rowan
Callick, 'Irian Jaya Rediscovered',
The Australian Financial Review, 18
January 1996, p. 15; Patrick
Walters, 'Troops Patrol Riot-torn
Irian Town', *The Australian*, 14
March 1996, p. 6; John McBeth,
'Now Hear This: Irian Jaya Rebels
Learn to Play Hardball', *Far
Eastern Economic Review*, 18 April
1996, pp. 24–25.
[26] See Imanuddin, 'Resentment
Triggering Unrest in Irian: Expert',
The Jakarta Post, 8 April 1996, p. 2.
[27] Patrick Walters, 'Crisis Claims 2
Million Casual Jobs in Jakarta', *The
Weekend Australian*, 3–4 January
1998, p. 9.
[28] Norman Myers, 'Global
Population Growth and Security',
paper prepared for the seminar
'Global Security Beyond 2000', pp.
16–17.

Chapter 3

[1] Hanns W. Maull, 'Energy and
Resources: The Strategic
Dimension', *Survival*, vol. 31, no.
6, November–December 1989,

p. 500.

[2] Paul Kennedy, *The Rise and Fall of the Great Powers: Economic Change and Military Conflict from 1500 to 2000* (London: Fontana Press, 1988); Jonathan Marshall, *To Have and Have Not: Southeast Asian Raw Materials and the Origins of the Pacific War* (Berkeley, CA: University of California Press, 1995).

[3] Henri Berenger quoted in Ronnie D. Lipschutz, *When Nations Clash: Raw Materials, Ideology and Foreign Policy* (Cambridge, MA: Ballinger, 1989), p. 74.

[4] Robert Mandel quoted in Richard Schultz, Roy Godson and Ted Greenwood (eds), *Security Studies for the 1990s* (New York: Brassey's, 1993), p. 347.

[5] Maddock, 'Environmental Security in East Asia', p. 27.

[6] Kent E. Calder, 'Policy Forum: Energy Futures', *The Washington Quarterly*, vol. 19, no. 4, Autumn 1996, p. 91; Ji Guoxing, 'East Asia's Energy Security', paper presented at the conference 'Asia-Pacific Security for the 21st Century', Honolulu, HI, 3–6 November 1997, p. 3.

[7] Daniel Yergin, Dennis Eklof and Jefferson Edwards, 'Fuelling Asia's Recovery', *Foreign Affairs*, vol. 77, no. 2, March–April 1998, pp. 35, 38.

[8] Kent E. Calder, *Asia's Deadly Triangle* (London: Nicholas Brealey Publishing, 1996), p. 50.

[9] Cambridge Energy Research Associates, *Asia-Pacific Energy Watch*, Winter/Spring 1997, p. 31.

[10] Yergin, Eklof and Edwards, 'Fuelling Asia's Recovery', p. 38.

[11] See Burnett, *The Western Pacific*, p. 116; and Calder, 'Policy Forum: Energy Futures', p. 92; Guoxing, 'East Asia's Energy Security', p. 3.

[12] *Asia 1995 Yearbook* (Hong Kong:

Far Eastern Economic Review, 1994), p. 51; *Asia 1997 Yearbook*, p. 54.

[13] Daniel Yergin, Dennis Eklof and Jefferson Edwards, 'Energy Security in the Asia-Pacific Region', paper presented at the IISS Annual Conference, Singapore, 11–14 September 1997, p. 6. The author is indebted to Daniel Yergin for permission to cite the data used in this paper.

[14] 'Japan Becoming More Dependent on Mideast Oil', *The Jakarta Post*, 14 February 1997, p. 10.

[15] Calder, *Asia's Deadly Triangle*, pp. 44–47.

[16] *Ibid.*, pp. 47–48.

[17] *Asia 1997 Yearbook*, p. 54.

[18] James P. Dorian, Brett H. Wigdortz and Dru C. Gladney, 'China and Central Asia's Volatile Mix: Energy, Trade and Ethnic Relations', *Asia Pacific Issues*, East–West Center Report No. 31, May 1997, p. 4; *Asia 1997 Yearbook*, pp. 54–55.

[19] Michael C. Lynch, 'The Nature of Energy Security', *Breakthroughs*, vol. 4, no. 1, Spring 1997, p. 4.

[20] *Ibid.*, p. 6.

[21] See 'Asia Vulnerable to Oil Supply Disruptions', *The Jakarta Post*, 31 October 1997, p. 10.

[22] Calder, *Asia's Deadly Triangle*, p. 54.

[23] Valencia, 'Energy and Insecurity in East Asia', p. 87.

[24] 'Regional Effort to Tap into Siberian Gas Field', *The Korea Herald*, 21 October 1997, http://nautilus.org/napsnet.

[25] Lyuba Zarsky, 'Energy and the Environment in Asia Pacific: Regional Cooperation and Market Governance', paper presented at a symposium on the UN system in the twenty-first century, United Nations University, New York,

14–15 November 1997, pp. 5–6.

26 Bruce and Jean Blanche, 'Oil and Regional Stability in the South China Sea', *Jane's Intelligence Review*, November 1995, p. 511.

27 Esmond D. Smith, 'China's Aspirations in the Spratly Islands', *Contemporary Southeast Asia*, vol. 16, no. 3, December 1994, p. 278.

28 Rigoberto Tiglao, 'Remote Control: China Expands Reefs to Extend Claims', *Far Eastern Economic Review*, 1 June 1995, p. 21.

29 Cited in Valencia, 'Energy and Insecurity in Asia', p. 96.

30 *Asia 1995 Yearbook*, p. 22.

31 Michael Vatikiotis, Murray Hiebert, Nigel Holloway and Matt Forney, 'Drawn to the Fray', *Far Eastern Economic Review*, 3 April 1997, p. 15.

32 'China Warned to Stop Drilling Near Spratlys', *The Jakarta Post*, 17 March 1997, p. 6.

33 Vatikiotis, Hiebert, Holloway and Forney, 'Drawn to the Fray', p. 14.

34 Kenneth L. Whiting, 'Gas-rich Islands Could be Next Point of Conflict', *The Sydney Morning Herald*, 18 May 1995, p. 14. Donald Emmerson, 'Indonesia, Malaysia, Singapore: a Regional Security Core?', in Richard J. Ellings and Sheldon W. Simon (eds), *Security Challenges in Southeast Asia: Enduring Issues, New Structures* (Armonk, NY: M. E. Sharpe, 1996), p. 13.

35 'Natuna Plan Must Run as Scheduled', *The Jakarta Post*, 27 July 1995, p. 1; 'RI Set to Start Development of Natuna Project', *ibid.*, 15 March 1996, p. 1.

36 Michael Richardson, 'Natural Gas is Prize in War Games', *The Australian*, 27 August 1996, p. 23. See also 'Armed Forces to Stage Major Military Exercises', *The Jakarta Post*, 21 August 1996, p. 2

and Patrick Walters, 'Indonesia to Stage Huge Exercise in South China Sea', *The Weekend Australian*, 24–25 August 1996, p. 16.

37 Discussions with senior Indonesian officials, Jakarta, September 1996.

38 See Clive Schofield, 'Island Disputes in East Asia Escalate', *Jane's Intelligence Review*, vol. 8, no. 11, November 1996, p. 518.

39 Paik Jin-Hyun, 'Territorial Disputes at Sea: Situation, Possibilities, Prognosis', paper presented to the 10th Asia-Pacific Roundtable, Kuala Lumpur, 5–8 June 1996, p. 3; Mark Valencia, 'China and the Law of the Sea Convention', *Business Times* (Singapore), 29–30 June 1996, p. 4.

40 Paik Jin-Hyun, 'Territorial Disputes at Sea', p. 3.

41 Ji Guoxing, 'The Diaoyudao (Senkaku) Disputes and Prospects for Settlement', *The Korean Journal of Defense Analysis*, vol. 7, no. 2, Winter 1994, pp. 293, 295.

42 Mark Valencia, 'Calming the Tokdo/Takeshima Controversy', *Business Times* (Singapore), 30–31 March 1996, p. 1.

43 Paik Jin-Hyun, 'Territorial Disputes at Sea', pp. 7–8.

44 M. J. McMillan and J. M. Silver, 'Nuclear Developments in the Asia and Pacific Region', *Australian Nuclear Science and Technology Organisation Report*, July 1993, pp. 4–8.

45 US Department of Energy (DOE) forecasts cited in Calder, *Asia's Deadly Triangle*, pp. 63–64.

46 For details of the US–North Korea agreement, see Barbara Opall, 'S. Korea Vies for Prime Role in Pyongyang Reactor Effort', *Defense News*, 6–12 March 1995, p. 16.

47 'South Korea to Build 16 New

Nuclear Power Plants by 2010', *AP-Dow Jones News Service*, 3 September 1997.
[48] Michael Richardson, 'Asian Nations Plan to Expand Horizons of Nuclear Power', *The Australian*, 16 January 1996, p. 9.
[49] See Michael Vatikiotis, Suhaini Aznam, Shin Jae Hoon and Lincoln Kaye, 'Stormy Passage: Japan's Plutonium Shipment Scares ASEAN', *Far Eastern Economic Review*, 8 October 1992, pp. 12–13; and Calder, *Asia's Deadly Triangle*, p. 67.
[50] 'Halt Nuclear Dumping, Japan Tells Russia', *The Age*, 19 October 1993, p. 8.
[51] 'DPRK Begins Construction for Taiwan's N-Waste', *Chosun Ilbo*, 23 July 1997, http://nautilus.org/napsnet; 'Taiwan Waste Shipments to North Korea Approved – Report', *AP-Dow Jones News Service*, 13 July 1997.
[52] Dennis Engbarth, 'Nuclear Waste Deal Threatens Reactor Plan', *The Weekend Australian*, 1–2 February 1997, p. 15; Charles S. Lee and Julian Baum, 'Radioactive Ruckus', *Far Eastern Economic Review*, 6 February 1997, p. 16.
[53] Chon Shi-yong, 'UN Opposes Taiwan's Nuclear Waste Shipment to DPRK', *Korea Herald*, 27 June 1997, http://nautilus.org/napsnet.
[54] Engbarth, 'Nuclear Waste Deal Threatens Reactor Plan'; Lee and Baum, 'Radioactive Ruckus', p. 16.
[55] 'Nuclear "Ploy to Undermine Beijing"', *South China Morning Post*, 30 May 1997, p. 10; Robert Garran, 'Beijing Friction as US Awaits Reply to Korea Peace Plan', *The Australian*, 16 April 1997, p. 8.
[56] Desmond Ball, 'Building Blocks for Regional Security: An Australian Perspective on Confidence and Security Building Measures (CSBMs) in the Asia/Pacific Region', *Canberra Paper on Strategy and Defence No. 83*, Strategic and Defence Studies Centre, Australian National University, Canberra, 1991, p. 78; Dennis Schulz, 'Danger by the Dozen', *The Bulletin*, 28 September 1993, pp. 16–18.
[57] 'House Approves Nuclear Power Bill', *The Jakarta Post*, 27 February 1997, p. 1; 'Indonesia Plays Down Pro-nuclear Power Program Legislation', *The Australian*, 28 February 1997, p. 1.
[58] Peter Landers, 'Nuclear Bombshells', *Far Eastern Economic Review*, 8 May 1997, p. 20.
[59] Jinzaburo Takagi, 'Japanese Nuclear Industry Aims at Asian Market', *The Jakarta Post*, 2 December 1997, p. 4.
[60] *Ibid.*

Chapter 4

[1] For a succinct account of the classical linkage between food and security, see Cheryl Christensen, 'Food and National Security', in Klaus Knorr and Frank Traeger (eds), *Economic Issues and National Security* (Lawrence, KS: University of Kansas Press, 1977), pp. 289–92.
[2] Nigel Holloway, 'No Pain, No Grain', *Far Eastern Economic Review*, 16 November 1995, p. 89.
[3] Lester Brown, *Who Will Feed China?*, p. 126.
[4] *World Resources 1994–95*, p. 107.
[5] Kevin Watkins, 'Why More Food Hasn't Helped the World's Hungry', *The Jakarta Post*, 26 October 1996, p. 5.
[6] *Ibid.*
[7] Paul Holmes, 'Realism to be Hallmark of World Food Summit', *The Jakarta Post*, 9 November 1996,

p. 5.
[8] 'Will the World Starve?', *The Economist*, 16 November 1996, p. 23. See also US Department of Agriculture figures cited in Holloway, 'No Pain, No Grain', p. 90.
[9] Paul Ehrlich quoted in David Suzuki, *Inside Story*, documentary, Australian Broadcasting Commission, 15 April 1997.
[10] Norman Myers, 'Environment and Security', *Foreign Policy*, no. 74, Spring 1989, p. 10.
[11] Julian Cribb, 'Grow or Die', *The Weekend Australian*, 1–2 July 1995, p. 26.
[12] *World Resources 1994–95*, p. 108.
[13] 'Philippines Places Rice Orders Ahead of El Nino', *The Jakarta Post*, 11 November 1997, p. 10.
[14] Michael Richardson, 'Timely Grain', *The Australian*, 12 July 1996, p. 25.
[15] Lester Brown, *Who Will Feed China?*, pp. 132–33.
[16] *Ibid.*, p. 134.
[17] *Ibid.*, p. 32.
[18] Smil, 'Environmental Problems in China', p. 36.
[19] *Ibid.*, pp. 30–31.
[20] *Economic Information Daily of China* cited in *ibid.*, p. 55.
[21] Jiang Chunyun quoted in Elizabeth Economy, 'The Case Study of China – Reforms and Resources: The Implications for State Capacity in the PRC', *Project on Environmental Scarcities, State Capacity and Civil Violence*, American Academy of Arts and Sciences and Committee on International Security Studies, University of Toronto, 1997, p. 14.
[22] *China Daily* cited in Richard McGregor, 'Beijing Propaganda Blast Defends its Growing Appetite', *The Australian*, 8 May 1996, p. 11.
[23] Richardson, 'Timely Grain'.
[24] Peter Hartcher, 'Facts Show Up Flaws in China Food Crisis Theory', *The Australian Financial Review*, 25 March 1997, p. 9.
[25] Julian Cribb, 'Cutbacks in Aid Jeopardise World Food Sufficiency', *The Weekend Australian*, 18–19 May 1996, p. 10.
[26] Nigel Holloway, 'No Pain, No Grain', p. 90.
[27] Brian Hunter, 'Looming Environmental Disasters: Where They are Now and How to Check Them', paper presented to the 11th Asia-Pacific Roundtable, Kuala Lumpur, 5–8 June 1997, p. 11.
[28] See Comprehensive National Security Study Group, 'Report on Comprehensive National Security', 2 July 1980, especially pp. 60–65.
[29] Terry Rambo, 'The Fallacy of Global Sustainable Development', *Asia-Pacific Issues No. 30*, East–West Center, March 1997, pp. 3–4.
[30] 'Will the World Starve?', p. 26.
[31] Cha Lim Sok, the Deputy Director of the Farm Produce Bureau of North Korea's Agricultural Commission, reported in January 1998 that 2.8m North Koreans had died from 'natural calamities' and that per capita food availability had declined to 180 grams a day. See '2.8 Million North Koreans Died from Natural Calamities', *Agence France-Presse*, 20 January 1998.
[32] See Teresa Watanabe and Hyungwon Kang, 'With a Bit of Ingenuity, North Koreans Find Food', *International Herald Tribune*, 10 June 1997, pp. 1, 6.
[33] UN World Food Programme estimates cited in Scott Snyder, 'A Coming Crisis on the Korean Peninsula?', *United States Institute of Peace Special Report*, 1996, pp. 10–11. See also 'CIA Warns of

North Korean War Threat', *The Australian*, 7 February 1997, p. 7.

[34] Nayan Chanda, Shim Jae Hoon and Peter Landers, 'On Borrowed Time', *Far Eastern Economic Review*, 26 June 1997, p. 23.

[35] Robert Garran, 'Desperate N. Korea Pleads for Food Aid', *The Australian*, 4 February 1997, p. 1.

[36] Caritas estimates cited in 'Aid Worker: N. Korea Hunger Grows', *The Associated Press*, 16 July 1997.

[37] Justin Jin, 'UN: For N. Koreans, Worst is Still to Come', *Reuters*, 28 October 1997. See also Andrew Browne, 'Caritas Warns Famine in N. Korea Far From Over', *ibid.*, 22 October 1997.

[38] Harvey Stockwin, 'Famine Struck Refugees Flee North Korea', *The Jakarta Post*, 13 February 1996.

[39] Dupont, 'Unregulated Population Flows in East Asia', pp. 15–16.

[40] *Human Development Report, 1994* (New York: Oxford University Press for the UN Development Programme (UNDP), 1994), p. 36.

[41] Geoffrey Lean, 'World Fisheries Now in a Sea of Trouble', *The Canberra Times*, 4 February 1995, p. C6.

[42] Trish Saywell, 'Fishing for Trouble', *Far Eastern Economic Review*, 13 March 1997, p. 51.

[43] Daniel Yarrow Coulter, 'South China Sea Fisheries: Countdown to Calamity', *Contemporary Southeast Asia*, vol. 17, no. 4, March 1996, p. 372.

[44] Eduardo A. Loayza and Lucian M. Sprague, 'A Strategy for Fisheries Development', *World Bank Discussion Papers*, no. 135, 1994, p. 2, cited in *ibid.*

[45] Saywell, 'Fishing for Trouble', pp. 50–51.

[46] Rear-Admiral R. M. Sunardi, Senior Adviser to Indonesia's Minister of Defence, quoted in Alan Dupont, 'Indonesian Defence Strategy and Security: Time for a Rethink?', *Contemporary Southeast Asia*, vol. 18, no. 3, December 1996, p. 280.

[47] *Asia 1997 Yearbook*, p. 56.

[48] *Ibid.* See also Kaji, 'Challenges to the East Asian Environment', p. 217.

[49] Saywell, 'Fishing for Trouble', p. 51.

[50] 'Protect Marine Resources', *The Jakarta Post*, 17 January 1997, p. 1.

[51] 'Fishing War Sows Conflict in Pacific Nations', *Korea Times*, 19 December 1989, p. 9.

[52] *Asia 1997 Yearbook*, p. 56.

[53] Mark Valencia, 'Asia, the Law of the Sea and International Relations', *International Affairs*, vol. 73, no. 2, April 1997, p. 268.

[54] Steve Lonergan, 'Environmental Change and Regional Security in Southeast Asia', *Project Report No. PR659*, Department of National Defence, Ottawa, 1994, p. 38.

[55] Gordon Fairclough, 'Floating Flashpoint: Fishing Fleets Aggravate Regional Tensions', *Far Eastern Economic Review*, 13 March 1997, p. 54.

[56] Michael Vatikiotis and Adam Schwarz, 'Crossed Lines: Thailand and Vietnam Clash over Fishing Rights', *ibid.*, 15 June 1995, p. 16.

[57] Fairclough, 'Floating Flashpoint', p. 50.

[58] 'Philippines Arrests Chinese and Taiwanese Fishermen in Disputed Waters', *Reuters*, 18 August 1997.

[59] 'RI loses $2bn a Year in Fishing Resources', *The Jakarta Post*, 8 August 1997, p. 2.

[60] 'Protect Marine Resources', *The Jakarta Post*, 17 January 1997, p. 1.

[61] 'Steps To Curb Poaching In Philippine Territorial Waters', *Central News Agency*, 6 August

1997, http://www.nautilus.org/trade.

62 'Fish the Real Booty in Spratlys: Experts', *The Jakarta Post*, 19 June 1995.

63 Juita Ramli, 'Malaysia and the Law of the Sea: A Harvest of Riches', *MIMA Bulletin*, vol. 4, no. 1, 1997, p. 3; Shee Poon Kim, 'China's Changing Policies Towards the South China Sea', *ibid.*, p. 26.

64 'ROK Plans to File Protest with PRC over "Piracy" Act', FBIS-EAS-96-110, 6 June 1996, p. 56.

65 'ROK: DPRK Incursion Possibly Done to Protect Fishing Boats', FBIS-EAS-96-116, 14 June 1996, pp. 31–32.

66 *Ibid.*

67 Mark Valencia, 'Asia, the Law of the Sea and International Relations', p. 273.

68 Ji Guoxing, 'The Diaoyudai (Senkaku) Disputes and Prospects for Settlement', p. 286.

69 Bruce Gilley, Sebastian Moffet, Julian Baum and Matt Foley, 'Rocks of Contention', *Far Eastern Economic Review*, 19 September 1996.

70 Geoffrey Till, 'Trouble in Paradise: Maritime Risks and Threats in the Western Pacific', *Jane's Intelligence Review*, Special Report No. 7, 1995, p. 10.

71 Schofield, 'Island Disputes in East Asia Escalate', p. 521; Valencia, 'Asia, the Law of the Sea and International Relations', p. 273.

72 Schofield, 'Island Disputes in East Asia Escalate', p. 518.

73 Robert Garran, 'Japan, South Korea Overlap in Claims for Economic Zones', *The Australian*, 21 February 1996, p. 9.

74 'Japan Denounced Over Fishing Dispute', *Korea Herald*, 15 July 1997, http://nautilus.org/

napsnet; 'S. Korea Parliament Denounces Japan', *United Press International*, 24 July 1997.

75 Son Key-young, 'Seoul Warns Tokyo of Grave Consequences in Bilateral Ties Over Fishing Disputes', *Korea Times*, 9 July 1997.

76 'Minister Yoo Rejects Japan's Demands on EEZ', *Chosun Ilbo*, 15 July 1997.

77 'Korea to Consider Temporary Fishery Deal with PRC', *Korea Herald*, 8 July 1997, http://nautilus.org/napsnet; Son Key-young, 'Cabinet Endorses Decree Banning Foreign Boats Fishing in EEZ', *Korea Times*, 30 July 1997, http://nautilus.org/napsnet.

Chapter 5

1 Peter Wallensteen and Ashok Swain, *International Fresh Water Resources: Conflict or Cooperation?*, Stockholm Environment Institute, June 1997, p. 4.

2 *Ibid.*, pp. 2–3.

3 See Vera Haller, 'Water an Issue at Food Summit', *The Jakarta Post*, 11 November 1996, p. 5.

4 Anthony Goodman, 'Only 0.007 Percent of World Water Found Usable', *The Jakarta Post*, 10 March 1997, p. 9.

5 *World Resources 1994–95*, p. 182.

6 Brown, 'Climate, Ecology and International Security', p. 124.

7 Wallensteen and Swain, *International Fresh Water Resources*, p. 4.

8 UN Population Fund, *Population, Resources and the Environment* (New York: UNFPA, 1991), p. 47.

9 Julian Cribb, 'Water Wars', *The Australian*, 15 January 1996, p. 12.

10 See Miriam R. Lowi, *Water and Power: The Politics of a Scarce Resource in the Jordan River Basin* (Cambridge: Cambridge

University Press, 1993), p. 1.

[11] Cited in Peter H. Gleick, 'Water and Conflict: Fresh Water Resources and International Security', *International Security*, vol. 18, no. 1, April 1991, p. 86. See also Joyce Starr, 'Water Wars', *Foreign Policy*, no. 82, Spring 1991, p. 17.

[12] Boutros Boutros-Ghali quoted in Natasha Beschorner, *Water and Instability in the Middle East*, Adelphi Paper 273 (London: Brassey's for the IISS, 1992), p. 3.

[13] *Ibid.*, p. 6.

[14] Cribb, 'Water Wars'; Juergen Dauth, 'WB Forecasts Water Crisis in Asian Countries', *The Jakarta Post*, 2 January 1997, p. 4.

[15] Philip Hurst, *Rainforest Politics: Ecological Destruction in Southeast Asia* (Kuala Lumpur: S. Abdul Majeed and Company, 1991), pp. xiii, 5.

[16] Maddock, 'Environmental Security in East Asia', p. 28.

[17] *Ibid.*, p. 433.

[18] Hurst, *Rainforest Politics*, p. xiii.

[19] Kaji, 'Challenges to the East Asian Environment', p. 211.

[20] Peter Dauvergne, 'Globalisation And Deforestation in the Asia-Pacific', *Working Paper No. 1997/7*, Department of International Relations, Australian National University, November 1997, p. 12.

[21] *World Resources 1994–95*, p. 73.

[22] Maddock, 'Environmental Security in East Asia', p. 28.

[23] Lonergan, 'Environmental Change and Regional Security in Southeast Asia', p. 63.

[24] *Ibid.*; Dauth, 'WB Forecasts Water Crisis in Asian Countries'.

[25] 'Water Crisis in 2005 Predicted', *The Jakarta Post*, 1 November 1995, p. 3.

[26] *Ibid.*

[27] 'Puncak Not Only Cause of Massive Floods', *The Jakarta Post*,

31 October 1996, p. 3.

[28] Adam Schwarz, 'Looking Back at Rio', *Far Eastern Economic Review*, 28 October 1993, p. 48.

[29] 'Puncak Not Only Cause of Massive Floods'.

[30] Burnett, *The Western Pacific*, pp. 155–56.

[31] Smil, 'Environmental Problems in China', p. 51.

[32] Brown, *Who Will Feed China?*, p. 66.

[33] These statistics and citations have been taken from Smil, 'Environmental Problems in China', p. 24; *World Resources 1994–95*, p. 73; and Economy, 'The Case Study of China', p. 21.

[34] Peter H. Gleick, 'An Introduction to Global Fresh Water Issues', in Peter H. Gleick (ed.), *Water in Crisis: A Guide to the World's Fresh Water Resources* (New York: Oxford University Press for the Stockholm Environment Institute, 1993), p. 6.

[35] 'India and Bangladesh: Sweeter Waters', *The Economist*, 16 November 1996, p. 26.

[36] Cribb, 'Water Wars'.

[37] Cited in Economy, 'The Case Study of China', p. 6.

[38] W. Harriet Critchley and Terry Terriff, 'Environment and Security', in Schultz, Godson and Greenwood (eds), *Security Studies for the 1990s*, p. 334.

[39] See Hurst, *Rainforest Politics*, pp. 197–200; Lim Teck Ghee and Mark J. Valencia (eds), *Conflict over Natural Resources in South-East Asia and the Pacific* (Singapore: Oxford University Press, 1990), pp. 44–45.

[40] Seth Faison, 'A Show of Power on Yangtze', *International Herald Tribune*, 10 November 1997, p. 1; Liang Chao, 'Blocking Yangtze: "No Problem"', *China Daily*, 8 November 1997, p. 1; 'Closing the

Last Gap, China Gives the Yangtze a New Course', *International Herald Tribune*, 8–9 November 1997, p. 1.
[41] See Scott Hillis, 'Three Gorges Dam, Eco-boon or Curse?', *The Jakarta Post*, 4 November 1997, p. 9.
[42] David Nelson, 'Toxic Waste: Hazardous to Asia's Health', *Asia-Pacific Issues Paper No. 34*, East–West Center, November 1997, p. 2.
[43] Irene Ng, 'Piping Up on Water Issues', *The New Paper*, 5 June 1997, p. 14.
[44] *Ibid.*; Jaqueline Lee, 'KL Uses Water as Political Tool', *The Jakarta Post*, 7 July 1997, p. 4.
[45] Kevin Hamlin, 'Singapore Seeks a Solution to Dependence on Imported Water', *Asia Times*, 11 June 1997, p. 3.
[46] 'Two States Likely to Exhaust Water Resources', *The Straits Times*, 11 November 1997.
[47] Ian Stewart, 'Apology Fails to Pacify Malaysia', *The Australian*, 17 March 1997, p. 7.
[48] Lee, 'KL Uses Water as Political Tool'.
[49] S. Jayasankaran and Murray Hiebert, 'Snipe, Snipe: Malaysia–Singapore Spat Reflects Growing Economic Rivalry', *Far Eastern Economic Review*, 5 June 1997, p. 24.
[50] 'PM Goh's Speech in Parliament: I Shall Work for a New Era of Cooperation', *The Straits Times*, 6 June 1997, p. 45.
[51] Kevin Hamlin, 'Singapore Seeks a Solution', p. 3.
[52] Data extracted from Table B.3, 'Lengths and Basin Countries of Selected Major Rivers, Four Estimates', in Gleick (ed.), *Water in Crisis*, pp. 151–52.
[53] Tony Gillotte, 'The Heart of the Mekong Threatened by Cambodia's Economic Surgery',

The World Paper, 23 November 1997, p. 1.
[54] Cisca Spencer, 'Challenge is to Tap Mekong without Being Damned', *The Australian*, 6 September 1996, p. 18.
[55] ADB figures cited in Michael Richardson, 'Harnessing the Mighty Mekong', *The Australian*, 28 April 1997, p. 24.
[56] Bertil Lintner, 'Cold-War Legacy', *Far Eastern Economic Review*, 10 August 1995, p. 30.
[57] Patrick Lescott, 'Asian Nations Sign Deal to Preserve Mekong', *The Australian*, 7 April 1995, p. 8.
[58] Richardson, 'Harnessing the Mighty Mekong'.
[59] Burnett, *The Western Pacific*, p. 148.
[60] Spencer, 'Financial Benefits to Flow from River Region Development'.
[61] William Barnes, 'Bonanza Dam Plan Threatens Mekong', *The Australian*, 15 December 1994, p. 4.

Conclusion

[1] See Dauvergne, 'Globalisation And Deforestation in the Asia-Pacific', pp. 9–10.
[2] Hanns Maull, 'Japan's Global Environmental Policies', in Andrew Hurrell and Benedict Kingsbury (eds), *The International Politics of the Environment* (Oxford: Clarendon Press, 1992), p. 355.
[3] Gareth Porter and Janet Walsh Brown, *Global Environmental Politics* (Boulder, CO: Westview Press, 1996), p. 1.
[4] Bron Raymond Taylor, 'Earth First! And Global Narratives of Popular Ecological Resistance', in Bron Raymond Taylor (ed.), *Ecological Resistance Movements: The Global Emergence of Radical and Popular Environmentalism* (Albany,

NY: State University of New York Press, 1995), pp. 14, 22.

[5] See, for example, Levy, 'Is the Environment a National Security Issue?' and Deudney, 'The Case Against Linking Environmental Degradation and National Security'.

[6] Magno, 'Environmental Security in the South China Sea', p. 109.

[7] 'Government Announces Names of River Polluters', *The Jakarta Post*, 31 October 1996, p. 1; 'China Closes 50,000 Polluting Factories', *ibid.*, 5 November 1996, p. 6.

[8] For other ASEAN environmental organisations, see Tommy Koh, 'The Environment in Southeast Asia: Prospects for Cooperation and Conflict', paper presented at the 'Fourth Southeast Asia Forum', Kuala Lumpur, 15–18 January 1992, pp. 5–6.

[9] Grant Hewison and Mohd Nizam Basiron, 'Marine Environmental Security', in Sam Bateman and Stephen Bates (eds), 'The Seas Unite: Maritime Cooperation in the Asia Pacific Region', *Canberra Papers on Strategy and Defence No. 18*, Strategic and Defence Studies Centre, Australian National University, Canberra, 1996, p. 154. See also Raja Malik Saripulazan Raja Kamarulzaman, 'ASEAN-

OSRAP: Strengthening Regional Capabilities', paper presented at the '1995 International Oil Spill Conference', Long Beach, CA, 27 February–2 March 1995.

[10] See Maddock, 'Environmental Security in East Asia', p. 29; *Asia 1997 Yearbook*, p. 56.

[11] 'Joint Statement, Asia-Pacific Economic Cooperation, Ministerial Meeting, Singapore', cited in Andrew Elek, 'Asia-Pacific Economic Cooperation (APEC)', *Southeast Asian Affairs 1991*, Institute of Southeast Asian Studies, Singapore, p. 47.

[12] Hewison and Basiron, 'Marine Environmental Security', pp. 147–63.

[13] See Lyuba Zarsky and Jason Hunter, 'Environmental Cooperation at APEC: The First Five Years', *Journal of Environment and Development*, vol. 6, no. 3, September 1997, pp. 243–48.

[14] Hewison and Basiron, 'Marine Environmental Security', p. 154.

[15] See, for example, Michael Harbottle, 'New Roles for the Military: Humanitarian and Environmental Security', *Conflict Studies*, no. 285, November 1995, p. 14; Kent Hughes Butts (ed.), *Environmental Security: A DOD Partnership For Peace* (Carlisle, PA: US Army War College, 1994), p. 2.